Lawyers, Lies and Labradors
One Woman's Search for Truth

BOOK POWER PUBLISHING

Lawyers, Lies and Labradors: One Woman's Search for Truth

Published by Book Power Publishing, A division of Niyah Press www.bookpowerpublishing.com

Book Power books may be purchased for educational, business, or sales promotional use. For more information, email support@bookpowerpublishing.com. You may also contact the author directly at keveney@keveneyevanne.com

ISBN: 978-1-945873-29-4

Memoir / Personal Development / Entrepreneurship

ONE WOMAN'S SEARCH FOR TRUTH

LAWYERS
LIES
and
Labradors

KEVENEY EVANNE

BOOK
POWER
PUBLISHING

DETROIT, MICHIGAN

For Grandma Evelyn:
My rock and my light, in this realm and beyond . . .

Advance Praise for
Lawyers, Lies and Labradors

"Reading this book is like sitting shotgun while Keveney speeds through in three years what takes most people a lifetime. With humor, courage, knowing, and honesty she reveals how both big and small events in one's life can be significant forces for change rather than becoming memories, scrapbooks, "what-if stories," or certificates. Lawyers, Lies and Labradors is full of liberation, love, laughter, and life-affirming lessons. The more personal her confessions and dreams, the more universal they become as teaching tools. She wanted to change the world as a lawyer but changed herself instead . . . and then her whole world changed."

– Michael Golden, Artist; Carmine, Texas

"Smart. Funny. Engaging. Downright life-changing. Keveney takes you on the trip of a lifetime. You feel like you're walking right there beside her as she takes a huge leap of faith to discover the power of love, acceptance, and universal truth. A must read. A must-take journey.

Keveney is the real deal, and you'll be touched by her amazing story of transformation; she just may inspire you to put aside your fears, hit the reset button, and live your best life."

– Jennifer Johnson, Concierge Realtor,
JLJohnson Properties; Houston, Texas

"With each word, I was transported on the shoulders of Keveney and all the characters within her story (including the furry ones).

The presence of ancient strength is the center of this book and the harnessing of Divine wisdom and trust flows through from beginning to end.

The transparency assisted me in understanding some lost aspects of my younger self allowing me to come full circle in many aha moments.

Thank you, Keveney, for allowing me into your journey and embodying your truth for us all to find and harness our own truth."

– Kimberly Ann Traecy, Owner and Creative Director, Big Red SEO, LLC; Omaho, Nebraska

"I stayed up late reading – I couldn't put the book down. It spoke to my soul."

– Jennie Fuller, Architect; Vallejo, California

"Lawyers, Lies and Labradors is a magical memoir filled with captivating stories of Keveney's adventures. I was pleasantly awakened to what I had forgotten to remember. It's a must read for anyone seeking a higher sense of self."

– Christina Tervay, Owner CMT Dezign; Spring, Texas

A Note from the Author

My highest purpose in this life is to spread Truth. Interestingly, my other goal has been to share my story. The irony is not lost on me.

These are the memories that define me, the stories that have shaped every aspect of my being and led me to this very moment. I've made every attempt to recount the events accurately and to describe the characters in my life with compassion and honesty. I also recognize that there were many friends (and even a few foes) playing their part, and they might tell their version a bit differently. That's ok; this is *my* story.

It's by no means my entire story, however. I want to point out that many people and events that are significant to me and have had a profound impact on my life do not appear on these pages. This by no means makes them less important to me, and their absence is merely a result of the stories not necessarily fitting into the narrative. I could have told countless tales of high school shenanigans, adventures with law school buddies abroad, and relationships that last a lifetime, but those belong in a different book.

With respect to people and their privacy, I've changed some names and identifying characteristics in this book. Some for reasons which will become clear in context and others out of respect for their anonymity.

Finally, I'd like to add that I'm a work in progress. I do not pretend to have all the answers. What I do know to be true is that I and I alone am responsible for my success and happiness (or lack thereof), and I have the power to change my circumstances for the better and seek the Higher.

And, the same applies to you, Truth Seeker.

Much love to all . . .
Keveney Evanne
November 17, 2019
Houston, TX

Foreword

MY NAME IS Heather Wells, Designer and Creator of LOVEthirteen Jewelry®. There are no accidents in life. In fact, the farther we get along down our path, the more the intricacy of this truth reveals itself. Meeting Keveney was one such moment.

I will always remember the childlike innocence of her eyes upon our first meeting. It was surprising because she was clearly a strong, intelligent woman of importance. As I worked with her through my crystal jewelry, beyond her turquoise green eyes of innocence was a deep and radiant soul who was completely open to receive. I suppose this is why her message came through so easily.

It has been my complete joy and honor to watch her shift her life in so many ways, to step into her gifts and genius. Keveney is a remarkable healer with such unusual gifts that play out so beautifully through animals. It is truly awe inspiring to not only watch her work with others, but to be on the receiving end of her enlightened gifts, as well. And now, by honoring her calling and her truth, she is inspiring others to do exactly the same!

Keveney is a dear and extraordinarily gifted friend, and it is an honor to know her, to call her a soul sister, and to watch her lead so many in pure light and love!

To all of you about to read this book, may you be blessed by Keveney's story and may something profound also awaken within you.

Many Many Blessings,
Heather Wells

Introduction

ALMOST EVERYONE TALKS to animals; very few people talk *with* animals.

I happen to be firmly planted in the second camp of people.

Before you read my story, let me paint a picture of what I do . . .

There's a term used to define that optimal state of consciousness when the Self vanishes and performance peaks. It's the moment when you become completely absorbed in what you're doing. Time and space disappear, and you're immersed in a feeling of energized focus and full enjoyment. Some researchers also call this a flow state or peak experience; others refer to it as the zone of genius. It's the most rewarding form of work you can do, so much so that it doesn't even feel like work. It's something that no one else can do quite like you. It's what makes you unique.

Unfortunately, some people go their whole lives without finding their flow.

This is where I come in.

I help people expand their consciousness, clear and tap into their intuitive channel, and find their flow—often with the help of animals. When most people hear what I do, they respond with something like "what?!" The thought of talking with animals is some sort of weird, supernatural sort of thing.

But it's true, my zone of genius is my ability to communicate with animals and receive the messages they send about their owners. It's what sets me apart from not only most people but from even the others who speak with animals. For me, animals aren't simply the other half of a conversation; they're our soul teachers and my conduit for healing humans.

You see, I've learned our external world is a perfect carbon copy of our internal energetics. Everything is energy, and we humans and our pets are energetic beings; the connection between our energy and our pet's is closely connected. Turns out our pets absorb a great deal of our energy and have so much that they want to tell us, but they lack the medium through which to communicate. Thus, they often manifest physical or behavioral issues as a result of our energy (and to get our attention). Animals can be the greatest teachers in our lives, if we listen to them. They know more about us than we think, and they can help us more than we can imagine.

My ability to communicate with animals allows me to help my clients achieve their prosperity goals from an approach that no one else can. The pets show me what is required to be healed, solved, and resolved in the human— be it a belief, current way of being, or past trauma. The coolest thing is that the improvements the human makes are then energetically returned to their animal. In fact, often the animal's physical ailments dissolve when the human's energy is cleared.

This means I have the privilege to serve as a channel to heal people through animals and, in turn, heal animals through people.

It probably goes without saying that I wasn't always in

this line of work. I didn't wake up one day and decide to start a business around talking with animals. Instead, I practiced law for ten years before I kicked the corporate grind and set out to monetize my passion. This book portrays many of the obstacles and challenges I had to overcome before I could find my true zone of genius. Ending my corporate career and beginning this magical phase of my life took letting go of a lot of old beliefs. I was filled with judgement, anger, doubt, and the need to be right. I needed to learn to embrace the power of forgiveness and gratitude.

Slowly, I become open to a new way of doing, being, and having. I had to learn that my thoughts and energy have the power to change my external world, and, yes, for me, I had to allow my mind to also hear the thoughts of animals.

I believe we come to this realm for one purpose: To realize and manifest our own divinity. We spend lifetimes seeking self-realization. Along the way, we have many opportunities to learn and expand. The past is for learning, and every moment of my suffering came with an offering.

My hope is that these pages will act as an inspiration to guide you through your own version of self-realization. I can't promise that your adventure will lead you to hold casual conversations with dogs; however, I promise it will help you find what you love and as an added benefit, trust that it can become a (very lucrative) living for you.

When your energy is clear and you're doing what you love, everything flows. Health, money, and relationships all seem to enter a state of harmony when you're doing the internal work and living in alignment with universal law (more on that later). I've helped many people follow in my footsteps: Kick the corporate grind and go beyond the corporate salary. I help them get more of what they want while doing what they love. My mission is to help you monetize your passion (perhaps with a little help from the animal kingdom).

One last thing I'll be upfront about: My life has been what some might call a little strange, and the book in your hands reflects that. Conversations I hold with animals are just the beginning. I could very well go on living a quiet existence, but I've decided to make my story known to the world.

If you're seeking to reach the highest version of yourself and hit your peak performance, then you'll likely find value in the story of my life thus far.

I'm sharing my truth to help you find yours.

CHAPTER 1
A Howl in the Night

❧

I DON'T KNOW WHAT I was dreaming about that night. I do know that at 3 AM, I awoke to an absolute nightmare. The sound that brought me crashing into reality was so harsh and loud that, at first, I thought our security alarm was going off. My heart raced at the thought that someone might have broken into our home. But in the next second, I realized that the sound was coming from the foot of my bed. It wasn't an alarm or another human I was hearing, but it was a horrible, blood-curdling scream.

I shook Raul, my husband, awake—he's a deep sleeper and didn't exactly jump into action in the heat of the moment like I did. I flicked on the light and rushed to the foot of the bed to see something that, to me, was worse than having an intruder in my home. The scream had come from my beloved dog, Kaspi. When I say "scream," I really mean it. I had no idea that a dog could make a sound like that. It was high, blaring, and laced with agony. I wanted to pretend she might be having a nightmare—you know, the ones where they twitch and whimper a bit or run in place as if they're chasing something like their life depends on it—but I knew it was more than that. So much more.

"Wake up, hurry, get your clothes on," I yelled.

Kaspi was a beautiful, snow white, Great Pyrenees and Labrador mix, and now, she was having a major seizure right before my eyes. She was as stiff and rigid as a board with her legs stretched out and her eyes rolled back in her head. She was foaming at the mouth and had defecated in our bed. I rushed to her sweet face, calling her name and trying to calm her, but there was nothing I could do against this seizure. This was hell.

You know how sometimes people say that a thought "struck them?" Well, what happened to me in that moment beside Kaspi was like that, only instead of a single thought, it was countless truths. All at once I was hit by this . . . gale force wind, a complete intuitive download of what was really happening. With that sudden rush, I knew with every cell of my body why this was happening to Kaspi—we did this to her.

It was our fault—the stress and anxiety we had been bringing into the home, the resistance, the anger. I'd been tracking negative energy into our house like mud on my Louboutins, and Kaspi was paying the price. It's easy for us humans to bury and bear the burden of life, to push down our feelings and move from one obligation to another, but there was no way for Kaspi to process it. All of this was killing our dog.

My mind became a swirl of guilt, shame, and fear. I was terrified that the problem had already gotten too far ahead of me. I saw the truth now, but was it too late?

Okay, Universe. I get it. Message received. I promise, if you let my dog live I will make changes today, right now. Consider it done. I'll fix this. Just let my dog live. Please.

As you can imagine, that conversation with the universe could have gone on a *lot* longer. You might say that I'm still having it today. I would have a lot of reflecting to do and a transformation to undergo, but for now I only had one job: Get Kaspi to the ER.

Since it was the middle of the night, our usual vet was closed. It would be a fifteen minute drive to the ER, and we weren't even out the door yet. I threw on clothes or perhaps it was just more presentable pajamas, I can't remember. Kaspi stopped seizing—at least for the moment—but remained rigid and unresponsive. Kinley, my other fur baby, watched all of this with wide, terrified eyes. She's a red Labrador who absolutely loved her big sister. Both Kinley and Kaspi were rescues, and Kinley came to us in pretty bad shape. We got her a few years after Kaspi, and Kaspi was her protector and security blanket. As it turns out, Kaspi may have been the only other dog Kinley really loved, which made their connection that much more special.

Kinley is a mommy's girl for sure, and she was doing everything she could to contribute to my efforts, running back and forth to give loving, supportive licks to me and Kaspi. It killed me to think about leaving her at a time like this, but I knew we couldn't take her with us to the ER. One sick dog was enough. Hoping to give her some semblance of comfort, I set out some peanut butter for her, hugged her, and told her everything was going to be okay. It must have been so traumatic for her to watch all of this unfold. She knew all was not okay.

Raul hoisted up all seventy-six pounds of Kaspi and moved for the bedroom door. Her legs were so stiff that I had to gently guide the process of getting her down the hall, holding her as we rounded corners, crossed the living room, and got outside. Once we were clear of the obstacle course that was the inside of my house, it felt like a mad sprint across the lawn to my husband's truck.

With a whole lot of effort, we got Kaspi into the backseat. I'd heard of people biting or choking on their tongues during a seizure, so we decided that my husband should ride in the back with her. That meant I would be driving, which was good because Raul was an absolute mess. His ability to think and speak coherently seemed to have left him. All he could do was fight back tears, hold Kaspi, and remind me to at least pause before blowing through stop signs and red lights.

Don't get me wrong. I was a mess, too, but just in a different way. I had tears in my eyes and a lump in my throat, but I knew that I had to hold it together if we were going to make it all the way to the ER.

The drive was a blur; I can only remember a few isolated moments. Kaspi remained mostly unresponsive, but occasionally her eyes rolled forward from the back of her head long enough to look at us and show that she was scared. I was in my head a lot, sorting through the truth. Deep down, I had known for the past few years that I was slowly killing myself. I just didn't know I was taking Kaspi with me. I was in a state of chronic anger and hate. My work in corporate law was eating me from the inside out. Raul and I were like ships passing in the night, barely touching or talking. Even our state of residence was getting me down. Texas was *murdering* my spirit. I was terrified that I might have already let this toxic environment fester too long for Kaspi to live through it. Was I too late? I glanced at Raul in the rearview mirror. He was trying his best to comfort Kaspi—talking to her and petting her in between moments of calm and more seizures.

"We have to change," I said. He, of course, was completely thrown off and confused by my remark. I wanted to go into greater detail and tell him everything I had seen, felt, heard, and now knew, but I realized this wasn't the time. For now, all I said was, "This is our fault."

The intuitive download I was experiencing was far from over. I was seeing the whole morning play out in my head.

We were going to make it to the vet. They were going to give us a diagnosis and talk through options. That was all well and good, and something inside me kept saying, "Bring her home and do what you did when you were little."

I'll explain the meaning of those words later.

I'm not sure if we *actually* came to a screeching halt in the ER drop-off, but that's the movie version, according to my memory. I got out of the car, ran into the lobby, and accosted the first staff member I saw. I was appreciative of the urgency they showed, and of all thoughts to have in that chaos, I remember thinking how interesting yet obvious it was that they would have a doggie-sized stretcher.

The things our minds churn out while in crisis can be so strange.

Once we got inside, it was time for them to take her away from us. I think, in that situation, anyone would want to be at their dog's side, but Raul and I knew that we would be in the way. We had to trust the doctors.

After all of the rushing, the breaking of the speed limit, the crying, the confusion, and the newfound clarity, the whole event came crashing down into an eerie silence. It was probably a little after 4 AM now, and the ER was working with a skeleton staff. Raul and I were stuck in the waiting room with nothing but our thoughts. We were almost as comatose as Kaspi. The woman at the desk kept offering us coffee and water; they seemed like far-off concepts that neither of us wanted.

Raul broke, "Am I going to lose my little girl?"

I knew the answer. Like many things I hear, feel, or inherently know, this was not an official medical diagnosis, but I knew it to be true. Kaspi would be coming home with us, alive. It was the hours, days, and weeks beyond her homecoming that were uncertain. The future could go either way, because it was up to us. Kaspi would come home, and we would be given a chance to save her. The only question was, would we be able to break our pattern before it was too late?

CHAPTER 2
Freshwater Mermaids

T HE MORE I thought about what was happening, the more I realized how far I'd come from the magic of my childhood and how that distance was killing me.

Step back to five-year-old Keveney. I'm walking down an old, rickety staircase built into a steep slope of grass and rock. The air is beyond clean, cool from the nearby fresh water and scented like the color green with a hint of fishy from the plant and aquatic life. It completely envelopes me. When I get to the bottom of the steps, I have a choice to make: Continue down six more crooked, steep cement steps and find myself on the pebble-covered beach of a beautiful lake, or I can turn and step onto a large deck leading to a wooden cottage. Let's start with the cottage.

Built into a hill on Keuka Lake in Penn Yan, New York, this little cottage was where my family and I would vacation to each July. Painted a deep, burnt red with an expansive porch framing two sides, the cottage was an open floor plan with essentially one big room and one big table for the entire family to gather around. Dad, Mom, Grandma Evelyn, Grandaunt Vonnie, Aunt Karen, my cousin Whitney, and a few other familial regulars came to this place to enjoy the simplicity of life—and it was indeed, very simple. There were two pull-out couches and a single rocking chair. We had a sink in the kitchen and one half-bath—a proper shower was an advancement that didn't come until I was a teenager. For most of my childhood, we took our baths in the lake—*environment, please forgive me for the soap, for I knew not what I did.*

It's strange to me how few comforts we had in that cottage, yet how comfortable it seemed. I don't think it's a coincidence that such a tight-knit family spent their vacations without a single wall between them, save the bathroom and a small changing space that was partitioned off with a curtain.

We played in the lake every day—all day—from sunup to sundown. My dad and I would often fish off the dock, and every now and then we'd take the boat for a quick ride, but the days mostly consisted of floating, swimming, and gliding beneath the waves. I was obsessed with the water; I think I learned how to swim before I could walk. If I could help it—with the assistance of a snorkel—I would spend twice as much time below the surface than above it. This leads me to the next magical realm, one that opened itself to me while I was beneath the surface of the lake.

For many years there was a floating dock out in the lake which also served as the perfect diving board (or deserted island depending on my mood as a child). I can't remember who removed it or why it disappeared—clearly the adults forgot to consult me! Although the dock was gone, the anchor that held it in place remained in the lakebed. This led to a new job that suited my interests very well. Before anyone could venture into the lake it was up to me to swim out, search for the anchor—yes, just like a deep-sea diver—and tie a warning buoy (a.k.a. an empty gallon milk jug) to it. Obviously, I took this job *very* seriously.

Once while I was out there doing my Jacques Cousteau

thing, I heard what sounded to me like a mermaid swatting her tail against the surface of the water. A fish? Most likely, I thought. Once I dove deep below the surface, I saw every little girl's ultimate fantasy. Beautiful and mysterious, she said four simple words, "You're one of us."

After I watched the mermaid swim away, I popped up to the surface and rushed to shore. Dripping and panting, I told my story to my dad. I'll never forget his reaction. He gave me the classic parental, "You're imagining things" line, with a little twist.

"Mermaids don't live in freshwater," he said.

But they do exist, was all I really heard in his response.

This sort of interaction is pretty typical of me and my dad, even today. I'm convinced I get my other-than-humanness from him.

Reality and fantasy tend to overlap in strange ways for me. Maybe it can all just be chalked up to childhood imagination, but there are enough synchronicities to make even my logical mind wonder if there was something more than fantasy to that underwater meeting with the aquatic goddess.

For example, I've always preferred water to land, and the butterfly kicks where you keep your feet perfectly together were my go-to. It felt like a more natural way to travel than kicking the usual freestyle manner and, for me, definitely better than the breaststroke. My tail-like leg behavior doesn't stop there. As an infant, my mom had to cut the feet off all my pajama suits or, apparently, I would scream. I think at some point she gave up and went with sleep gowns. To this day, I don't tolerate close toed shoes well; you will never find me in a pair of sneakers (thank goodness for yoga, Pilates, and, of course, swimming). Honestly, I prefer bare feet no matter the occasion—flip-flops are an okay compromise, and I've been known to wear them through even a foot of snow.

One more mermaid oddity: Although I don't consider myself a car person—I couldn't care less about horsepower, spoilers, or trends—there is one car that I am a bit obsessed with and will buy one day: a Maserati. It's not the performance, ultra-luxury, or sleek style that revs my engine. It's much simpler than that. It's the trident logo, which I immediately likened to Poseidon's spear (an association I owe to Disney's *The Little Mermaid*.) I've been drawn to that logo ever since my nine-year-old self first laid eyes on it in New York City.

Believe it or not, my maybe encounter with a mermaid was not the most memorable thing of those summer trips to the lake. As many people say, "It was the little things." Keuka Lake was about mini-golfing in the late evening, getting watermelon sherbet on the way home with my dad, swimming up and down the lake with my mom, and painting with watercolors on rocks with my gram. Keuka Lake has so much meaning to me—it means family, fun, and lots of love. Whether we were swimming in the water or sitting around that huge table playing card games with everyone— even Grandaunt Rosie who loved to cheat and always got caught—the lake during summers was my happy place.

At night, my mom and Aunt Karen claimed the pull-out couches inside. This was fine with the rest of us because even though we had a perfectly good shelter at our disposal, we preferred to sleep on the porch. My dad's snoring was notorious, some joked it could likely be heard all the way across the lake. Nights at the cottage were also defined by our campfires and the stories that were told around them. Most of the time, the storyteller was my dad, and his stories were otherworldly and contrived with an intent to scare my younger cousin, Whitney. Sometimes though, when my dad would take a break from this role, we'd hear tales of days gone by. This leads me to the next magical realm of Keuka Lake, although it isn't a place—it's a person.

Then and now, my Grandma Evelyn was both my rock and my light. She brought an incredibly grounded yet optimistic flair to every trip. I always had a deep connection with her, one that continues to this day even though she's no longer with us in physical form. Typically, we would celebrate both of our birthdays at the lake since hers was July 15th and mine the 12th. It was just one more thing that bound us together, along with other things like our incredibly flat feet, extreme independence, and cutting off the nose to spite the face stubbornness.

My grandpa passed away when I was only six months old, leaving Grandma Evelyn to her own devices. Despite living alone for over 30 years, she never seemed lonely. I like to think I filled the space in her heart that my grandpa left when he died. As for what magic she worked on my heart, it's difficult to put to words.

Since I was a teenager, I'd talk to Grandma almost every day and at least once a week even when I'd travel abroad for months at a time. At the lake, though, we were attached at the hip; like me, she couldn't get enough of the water. I can still see the sun reflecting off of the lake and lighting my grandma's eyes when she laughed. Each night, as we lay down to sleep—she on a porch glider and me on my air mattress next to her—I would practically beg her to tell stories about the olden days. Life back then was so interesting to me; I have a connection with those times that we'll get into later. Grandma grew up on a farm, plucking chickens for her parents. She would tell us all about the work and the smell that came with it, things that blew my mind considering we bought our chickens boneless, featherless, and skinless— other than the shrink wrap that swaddled them. (Sidebar, I'm now a vegetarian—you won't see anything with claws, paws, feet, hooves, or fins on my plate.) The absolute craziest thing to me was that she grew up using only an outhouse. I had this obsessive curiosity over the fact that she used to have to put on shoes—or worse, boots—every time she wanted to go to the bathroom.

My favorite story of hers made me feel like she was the bravest woman in the world. One night, Grandma was driving home with her two little girls that I now call "mom" and "aunt" in the back seat when a powerful storm by the name of Hurricane Hazel swept over town and through the northeast. The wind was so fierce that it had knocked a tree down and ripped free a power line right in the road in front of her. She stopped the car and watched as the live wire sparked and flipped around like an angry serpent.

At that moment, she knew two things: She needed to get my mom and aunt home before the wind blew an unlucky tree hard enough to send it crashing down on the car, and the only way home was to get past the aforementioned electric snake in the road. This left her with only one option.

She took a deep breath.

She watched the cable as it blew up, then down, then up again.

She found a rhythm to its motion and started to count the seconds between lifts and drops. When the time was right, she threw the car into gear and went cruising forward. Spoiler—they went right under the wire and all three wonderful women survived to tell the tale. This was one of the many ways that she was brave—another can be found in how she viewed things like death, souls, and the afterlife.

"I don't know what happens when people die, but they're dead, so leave them alone." She said that frequently, never without a smile. That was my philosophy for a long time—who could possibly know anyway—but my understanding of what lies beyond only developed further from there. As ironic as it was, that courageous woman who couldn't worry less about post-mortem existence would be the one who helped me expand my knowledge in this area the most, and she would do it after she was gone.

CHAPTER 3
The Healer and the Thief

I BELIEVE CHILDHOOD IS our root system, it's deeper than just our past. Many of us know and understand a lot more when we're little than we do after we're grown. If we're lucky—or disciplined and committed—we can come full circle as adults and find those natural Truths that we understood as children. If you're unhappy in life or feel as though you're missing something, one easy way to put a smile on your face is to seek out something that made you happy as a kid, and *do it*.

Growing up in Huntingdon, Pennsylvania, my life involved much of what it involves today—communicating with pets and healing and serving the world. I used to love making my special healing potions by flipping a Frisbee upside down, filling it with mud and mixing in flowers to give it its magical properties. Everyone around me was the fortunate recipient of my healing concoctions at one point or another. My good friend, Gretchen, had her share, and my dog, Maggie, got constant coatings of flowery Frisbee mud on her paws. I'm sure she was much better off for it. Dominic, my best buddy, was subjected to the same medical treatments—probably more than any of my other patients.

I can only assume his mother *loved* me for routinely sending her son home covered in dry mud and flower petals.

I wanted to solve all of the world's problems. And, at eight years old, I thought I could really do it—all with the power of my magic tinctures and tonics. Obviously, a task as big as that would require an awful lot of potion, and luckily I knew just where to get my supplies. My neighbors maintained a beautiful garden of herbs, flowers, tomatoes—everything a young healer like myself needed. Too much for one little girl to carry, I convinced Gretchen to carry out a heist for the greater good by sneaking out and raiding the entire garden of its valuable materials.

We slipped through the hedge between the houses and, under cover of darkness, we took everything we could carry . . . everything. We then brought it back to the hiding place that we had pre-selected. There was my old kiddie pool in my dad's shed, along with all the other items you would expect to find there like our lawnmower and gardening tools. Gretchen and I dropped the score in the pool, covered it up, and fled the scene as fast as possible. There was only one problem with this plan—in the coming days, I was so terrified of being caught that I couldn't bring myself to go back into the shed and use any of my supplies. So there they sat, until the day my dad decided it was time to mow the lawn.

I heard my name called in the way that could only mean trouble. When I was questioned about the neighbor's stolen goods, I tried to play the crime off on the two, older trouble-maker boys that lived across the street. My parents were still a little upset with them for putting our male and female pet rabbits in the same cage, resulting in an enormous family of little bunnies. I didn't mind having the cute little fury ones around, but I knew it was a prank—maybe this could be considered a prank, too?

No dice.

My parents were already well aware of my obsession with flowers and the like.

They passed the word to Gretchen's mom so that justice could be served to all guilty parties, but I knew she would be fine. Her older sister tended to get grounded for a month but be back out on the town the next day. I would be the less fortunate of the two. On the rare occasions I got punished, the punishment stuck. My feelings on the matter of punishment were probably different back then, and now I can see that Gretchen not being allowed to come play for a week after absolutely ransacking someone's hard-cultivated garden was a fairly light sentence.

My having to play alone for a week wasn't the worst part. Because my parents were not without a sense of poetic justice, they drove us to Gretchen's uncle's nursery and made us pick out all new flowers and deliver them to our neighbors as a peace offering. Obviously, this was a terrifying experience for me. I recall them both as being old and unsmiling, not necessarily angry, but definitely not happy. They were simply straight-faced and stoic, trying to scare us into knowing that we did wrong. I can't say I blame them for that.

The whole series of events led to a pretty dramatic shift in my healing operation. I had officially learned that some prices, such as looking into the eyes of those stoically disappointed elders, were indeed too high to pay in the name of my world-healing endeavors.

Still, my love of flowers and intuitive understanding of their healing properties permeated every aspect of playtime. I had a make-your-own perfume set that came with various scented fluids, but no flowers. I was quick to remedy that little shortcoming and soon every Keveney brand perfume came with a dose of my signature ingredient, be it dandelions, rose petals, or lilacs. Flowers were a must.

Now, for serving the world, literally. Dominic and I both shared a desire to feed the hungry. We were well below the age of doing any real cooking or using cutlery, so we did our best with what we had at our disposal. I would drag all of my mom's dishes out of the house during business (or completely random) hours for a restaurant that we co-founded. It was called "Hawaiian Hunger," and we never quite managed to feed anyone considering how sparse the menu was—mostly just salad, and by "salad" I mean grass. Even then each plate needed to be garnished with a flower, hand-selected by me of course (not entirely sure if all were edible).

There are countless things that sent me down that path of healing and serving—some known by me and others that I'll never understand—but I think one thing that sends us all down our respective paths is our parents. Both of mine were similar enough to be in love and different enough to keep my childhood interesting. My mother tended to call the shots and was the disciplinarian. She was a tenured professor at a liberal arts college; her position was secure and her income stable. And that's exactly what she wanted for me—steady income from a normal, respectable profession. Obviously, I've ended up a few miles shy of "normal" (she jokes about her lawyer daughter turned "psychic"), but I know that the way she raised me helped me to find myself at the right time. Just imagine where I would be right now if I immediately took out a business loan and opened up the real-life version of "Hawaiian Hunger." Fortunately, I had a very pragmatic woman in my life keeping me from leaping before I looked.

While my mother was on the ground attempting to fix problems even before they happened, my dad liked to dream. He encouraged me to do absolutely anything I wanted—although apparently raiding the neighbor's garden was not an option. He is a man of few words, and, for most of his life, was surrounded entirely by women. Our closest family members consisted of me, my mother, my aunt and her daughter, and, of course, Grandma (not to mention my dad grew up with three sisters). For the most part, my father remained the only man at holiday gatherings until I married Raul. Like me, he's pretty mild mannered . . . until he's not.

I've always been close to both my parents. During the summer, Mom and I spent most days at the country club pool. During the school year, from first to fifth grade anyway, my dad picked me up almost every day and took me to lunch; this was our special time together.

My dad is the quirky one for sure, and he had this lovable desire to bring his weirdness into my life. His running joke while driving was to suddenly shift the car into low gear and claim that the jolt was an alien invasion taking us off to our homeland—this happened every time we went through Dairy Queen when my cousin visited and always ended with her in sheer terror and tears. He loved *The Hobbit,* and he insisted on reading it to me at every opportunity he had. The only flaw in this plan was that I had absolutely no desire to listen to Bilbo's journey . . . I was five. I couldn't stand fantasy—couldn't be bothered to watch his sci-fi TV shows. For a long time, I thought this was just a matter of taste and interest. Who could judge a little girl for liking flowers more than aliens and goblins? Now, I realize it went way deeper than just personal preference. My own, real world was far too magical for any fiction to interest me.

I already had enough imagination in my life—I didn't need to get it from a page or a screen. TV of any kind never had much of a draw for me. To this day, I'm still rocking an old, 80-pound, takes-up-the-entire-corner, sorry-excuse-for-a-television in my living room. It's under-used—which maybe is just the right amount of use—but serves a great purpose as our home security system. Anyone looking through the glass doors in my backyard will see that dusty piece of ancient technology sitting there and know that there is nothing in my living room worth their time.

The fact that I own this antique theft deterrent can definitely be traced all the way back to my fantastical childhood. Falling asleep alone was a constant struggle because I was always seeing things move around me in the dark. I saw things, I knew things, I felt things, and I was already developing a strong connection with animals. In one instance, while cleaning up after the bunnies we kept in our backyard, I finished scraping up the rabbit poop around their pens, and wanted to keep raking—not raking really, but digging. I knew without a doubt that I had to get down there, dig, and dig, until I found—what?

"Oh, what are you going to find down there, a body?" My father asked, with just a little bit of laughter. No sooner did I brush a patch of dirt away to find what looked like a baby's foot sticking out of the ground.

Okay, technically it wasn't human, but human-shaped and, at one time, skin-colored. It belonged to an old baby doll that had been buried long before I was born—before my family even moved into the house—forty years, to be specific. We didn't learn that exact number until word of the doll's recovery made it to Gretchen's mom. It turns out, Gretchen's mom used to live in our house when she was my age. Her mischievous brother had apparently stolen her sister's doll and buried it in the yard for some reason or another without ever fessing up to her about it. I guess you could glean from this that love always wins, even if it takes the intuition of one little girl a generation later to bring things full circle. When I returned the doll to Gretchen's aunt, she was in awe.

Sometimes it wasn't as simple as knowing things, and sometimes I wasn't the only one involved. In one instance, it came down to the very-real experience of seeing something with my own eyes. It might be more interesting to tell this one from my mother's perspective, who had been downstairs when Dominic and I came running down to her shouting that there was a strange man in the house. A rational thinker, my mom asked us to describe the intruder.

My friend and I had been prone to imaginary ghost sightings in the past, always ending up with a different description of the apparition—not this time. Both Dominic and I gave the same answer, telling her about the man's round-brimmed hat. We had both seen the same person standing on the stairs. So, my mom suggested we all go wait outside, and she called my dad to come home. Looking back, I wonder if she and my dad were only appeasing us because it's not like she called the police.

Of course, once my dad arrived there was no sign that anyone had broken into the house. Even if they had, how and why would they come into the second story of the house during broad daylight? My mom rationalized that we must have mistaken a hanging wreath at the top of the staircase for a man's hat. I'm not sure what my dad thought—like I said, he is a man of few words who believes in aliens and orcs—and likely ghosts, too.

Everywhere I looked I saw life where others couldn't. It was the summer before first grade when I saw one particularly special instance of this hidden life. While out flower shopping with my mom and grandma, I walked past a garden gnome. He was about a foot tall, holding a bunny, and looking innocent and wise, as those delightful lawn ornaments tended to appear to my younger self. This wasn't his most alluring quality, though. Out of the corner of my eye, whenever I wasn't looking directly at it, I could see the gnome move. He wasn't pulling a full-blown *Toy Story* by walking around. In fact, every time I looked back at him, he was standing in the same position. The motion was subtle, but it was there—and I was the only one who could see it. I was convinced that if I could just take him home, I'd be able to communicate with him. He could be my BFF when Gretchen and Dominic weren't around or when my dog became fed up with my frolics for the day. Maybe, once we got him out of the store, he would be free to come fully alive—like the Pillsbury Doughboy I so adored from the commercial.

I did not want for anything growing up. If possible, my parents got me anything that I asked for, sometimes even when they couldn't afford it. So, I don't know if she did this reluctantly or happily, but I do know that my mom bought me the gnome on that day. It's hard for me to explain the childhood excitement I felt over bringing home a real, living, mythical being to live in the backyard. I knew just where to put him, too.

Hidden in the back of our yard near my dad's shed, nestled under a tall tree was just enough dirt for a small flower garden. I always picked the flowers for this spot, and I was not about to plant more marigolds which seemed to be my parents' flower of choice. I was incredibly drawn to pansies and always planted them here. It should be noted that these particular flowers were off limits for potions as they were beloved to the fairies, and you don't want to upset the fairies as they can be quite tricky. This was my little sanctuary— my potion-making station. And, it was the perfect home for my new gnome friend, whom I named "Guy" after a tiny guinea-pig/mouse-looking stuffed animal I carried around the way most kids cling to a binky (coincidently, he was dressed much like my gnome with blue trousers, a red shirt, and a pointy hat). Once Guy the Gnome was placed in the fairy garden, he played the role of the wizard in laboratory. He presided over all of my playtime activities and kept me company during my brief retreats from the rest of the world. Dominic still teases me about that gnome.

I would later find out that like the pansies, I had a much more significant connection to gnomes than I realized. At that time though, the only hint I had of this tether between myself and gnomes was the fact that my new friend would visit me in my dreams. Back then, I mostly took dreams at face value—they were dreams. Today, knowing what I know, I can't help but think there was something more to them, a glimpse into another dimension or parallel universe perhaps.

It's no wonder to me why I found things like *The Hobbit* and *Star Trek* to be boring wastes of times (still do). Real life was simply way too magical. Rather than sit in front of a TV screen, I preferred to be in my garden—or to stand in front of the huge blackboard we had in our laundry room. That was where I would play teacher, setting up a classroom full of toys and imparting my childhood (or ancient, who really knows) wisdom on them. I think it's very telling that my baby dolls were never a part of the student body—only my stuffed animals. I had more interest in communicating with them than I did with pretend humans. I suppose this also ties into the exceptions I made around watching TV. For a time, I would only watch *The Little Mermaid, The Smurfs,* and *Lady and the Tramp* . . . a pretty fitting lineup for a young mermaid that can communicate with pets and whose favorite friend is a gnome.

This brings me to Maggie. She was a wonderful mutt that resembled a border collie and who no doubt played a major role in my desire to become the next *Doctor Doolittle*—another exception in my television embargo. I loved playing dress-up with Maggie. Thanks to my fashion eye, she got to experience wearing bonnets, bows, t-shirts, and shorts. She was like one of my baby dolls, only I could communicate with her. Even when I was playing teacher, Maggie was there, patiently playing the role of student, eager to learn my lessons.

We weren't immediately close, though. Maggie was about a year old when I was born, and the attention that I drew as a newborn baby inspired a little bit of sibling jealousy in her. I mention this only because it illustrates how desperate animals can be to communicate with us, even when they're surrounded by people who can't understand them. To cope with her jealousy and to draw some attention, Maggie actually tried chewing her tail off. Gruesome, I know, but it just goes to show how much Maggie was feeling and how little she was being heard.

As I grew older, I think one of my first overly intense connections with Maggie was pushed through by two powerful emotions—anxiety and fear. It happened when my father was cutting Maggie's nails, which was an extremely delicate procedure—cut too high, and you can end up hurting the dog or even drawing blood. In those days, I thought that even the smallest of cut to the quick would inevitably lead to death by bleeding. In my mind, it would be a vicious rush of blood that could not be stopped. So, knowing full well that this pedicure could result in the death of my favorite creature, I was feeling a little high-strung (you can see, I had zero tendency to exaggerate as a child).

I was horribly anxious, and I could tell that Maggie was picking up on it. With images of her getting hurt dancing around in my mind, Maggie must have been seeing them and getting stressed—possibly even more stressed than me. At one point it was like a little rubber band of stress in me snapped. I flinched, Maggie jumped, and my dad cut a little too high on one of her nails. She started bleeding. That was the end of it, I killed my dog. She would bleed to death and I would have to run away, never see my parents again, never look them in the eyes. It would be all my fault.

My panic fed into Maggie's fear, which added chaos to the environment, which no doubt freaked my dad out beyond belief. I remember Billy Joel's "River of Dreams" was playing in the background for that entire nightmare scenario, and all these years later whenever that song comes on, my dad and I share a subtle, knowing look . . . of sheer terror.

As I grew older, my ability to communicate with Maggie grew more refined and, thankfully, much safer. Once I discovered that some animals communicate using pictures, it was easier to strengthen my connection with Maggie. I would close my eyes tight, scrunch my face, and clench my hands into shaking fists. My internal process of visualizing the images before sending them, although I didn't know the name for it at the time, was utilizing my third eye, also known as the eye of insight. I can only imagine what my response would have been back then if someone told me that I was activating a place of power and wisdom in my forehead whenever I played with my dog.

We had this game that we would play where I would set up all of my toys on the couch—stuffed animals on one side, baby dolls on the other. If I sent her pictures of the animal side, she would go up to them, give them a sniff, and return. The same held true for the baby doll side. It was like playing a silent game of Simon Says.

As you can imagine, for a girl that wanted nothing more than to be Doctor Doolittle when she grew up, this ability to tell my dog where to go was thrilling. On top of that, I always wanted to be able to move things with my mind. This is something that I've never been able to do, but as a child I thought that's what I was doing to Maggie. Now, I realize this wasn't mind control at all—these were requests, and Maggie just happened to be a very accommodating dog.

Sadly, none of these abilities stood a chance against the

process of growing up in our current world. The more the grown-ups talked, the more I started to believe that having Doolittle's powers was nothing but a fantasy. I don't blame anyone in particular, like I said, the removal of magic is just a product of that slow transition we all make towards adulthood. It's our environment and society that strip us of these natural abilities and instincts.

In middle school and high school, I was a well-adjusted and happy teen—an officer in student council, editor of the yearbook, sweet boyfriend, college-bound, host of the best parties, all that jazz. I was friends with everyone from the preppy, popular crowd to some "misfits." Those more unique friends of mine were very much like the magic that I had in my world. They were special to me and very positive presences, but the popular crowd was louder. The less accepting teens and adults warned me about the dangers of hanging with the "wrong" people. Slowly but surely, under all of that adolescent pressure, I distanced myself from what was "different" and unknowingly entered a mundane existence with a narrow reality (and—yes—it felt as heavy as it sounds).

Just because I didn't see these other neighboring realms didn't mean they had left me, though. There was one incident, even after I had turned my back on magic, that the universe tried to remind me there was more to it than what my own eyes could see.

It happened in ninth grade.

I was on a club trip to Valley Forge, Pennsylvania, with fellow Key Club members. It was a three-day convention for high school students across the state to come together to celebrate service and leadership. It was the last night of the trip and three of my girlfriends and I were taking the elevator from our hotel room down to the ballroom for the final dinner and reception. When we got downstairs, I realized I had forgotten my name tag, which meant I wouldn't be able to get into the party. So, I stayed on the elevator to ride it back up while my friends waited for me in the lobby.

As the doors closed, I had no idea that my fate was sealed; I would not be attending the formal . . . at least not on time.

The elevator climbed and when the doors opened, I found that I was no longer in the Valley Forge Convention Center. Stepping off of the elevator, I saw a sign to my left that said, "Oasis Bar and Grill." There was definitely no establishment by that name in the convention center.

I didn't dare step into the bar, but from the hallway, I beheld a scene that was completely out of time. The sounds of a saxophone from a live jazz band came drifting out to me. The entire wait staff were Black, and the crowd was strictly White. I intuitively knew that, wherever and whenever I was, segregation was still in existence. The staff was not being treated well, and in this time, that was acceptable.

I backed away from the bar and looked down the hallway that held the hotel rooms. Each room number was marked by a cutout of a wooden cactus—definitely not the convention center's chosen aesthetic. At the time, I ignored that fact and walked down the hallway, hoping to break through the confusion and find my room.

It was too weird. The deeper I went down the hallway, the worse I felt. Turning back the way I came, I ran into a member of the wait staff who was pushing a room service cart. He was wearing black slacks and an off-white blazer with black trim. Definitely not modern attire.

I was so relieved to see an adult, and I immediately started asking for help. "Excuse me, sir," I said, trying to remain calm. He wouldn't make eye contact with me, and I saw that he was afraid of me. "I'm trying to get back to the Valley Forge Convention Center. I'm attending the conference with the other students."

"Ma'am," he said, his southern drawl coming through clear as day. "I don't know what you're saying. This is the Oasis Bar and Grill Hotel. I haven't heard of any convention center."

The man was an upsetting blend of confused and couldn't help. He looked toward me as if I had two heads; thinking back, I'm sure I appeared the same to him.

I started to panic and ran back to the elevator. It was gone, replaced by only a blank wall. I found the stairs, which I had taken many times at the convention center, and headed down for the lobby in desperate hope that my friends would be there waiting for me.

When I reached the bottom, I was confronted by a locked door with a narrow slat of glass running down its right side. On the other side of the glass, I could see a seedy, dark lobby with a reception desk. Beyond that was a door to the outside. A mysterious voice in me spoke up.

If you go out there, you will never get back.

I started hyperventilating and ran back upstairs to the strange bar.

There was a woman up there, waiting for me. She was also Black. Robust, strong, and wearing a deep purple, double-breasted cape-like overcoat. Black buttons, black shoes, black purse. Her presence was both calming and overwhelming.

"Honey," she said. "Come with me. I'll help you."

Just when I wondered how anyone could possibly help me in this situation, she said, "I'm going to take you back."

She took me to the wall where the elevator was supposed to be, and I noticed subtle bands of what could be called a fluidic rainbow—like grease on a wet road. She walked me through the strange spectrum of colors, and after that, I remember very little.

"You're gonna be okay now."

The next thing I knew, my friend's mom, one of the chaperones, was standing over me in the convention center lobby. Everyone was upset, they had all been looking for me. Even hotel security was there.

They told me later that when the elevator door opened, I was in a fetal position in the corner of the elevator, curled up in my ball gown. When they pulled me out into the lobby, I wondered why they were so worried; I figured I had only been gone for about ten minutes.

They told me I was gone for over an hour. They had spent most of that time going up and down the same elevator, the steps, and searching the halls. Yet, I was nowhere to be found.

I calmed down enough to start saying, "I want to call my mom," over and over again. In that initial call, even though she was happy to listen, she was certain that I was just messing with her. The trip was well-chaperoned, and everyone knew that drugs or alcohol weren't at play. I hadn't had so much as an aspirin.

It was in the many calls and conversations to follow that she began to believe me.

"You had a tendency to exaggerate things," she would one day tell me. "But whenever you tell that story, it's the exact same every time, like it happened yesterday."

It was one of the most mysterious experiences of my life, and I wouldn't find out its true meaning until well into adulthood.

I'm sorry to say that from here forward, although I had my highs and lows, I only grew more distant from my own personal joy and wonder. It was hard to notice at first, but things began to take a downward turn as I grew older. It was a spiraling negative pattern, culminating with a family tragedy that knocked me completely off the rails. As dark as the coming chapters are, they're equally important. You might say they're the reason I felt compelled to write this book: To help you catch the spiral before I caught mine.

CHAPTER 4
Legally Confused

❧

THINGS WENT PRETTY smooth for a while after childhood. As my dream of becoming the next Dr. Doolittle faded out of existence, it was supplanted by an aim to become another silver screen superstar, Clarice Starling from *Silence of the Lambs*. Quite a leap, I know. I went off to study politics and psychology at Muhlenberg College in Allentown, Pennsylvania, and loved it . . . my first year. For a small college, Greek life was a big deal. Thankfully, freshmen weren't permitted to pledge so I didn't have to worry about it in the beginning. Looking back, I don't even remember why sororities and fraternities irked me so much. By the time I became a sophomore, I had a real axe to grind against them. I can see now that I'd always been one to fight against institutions, sometimes if only for the sake of the fight. I can also see where I was not aligning with spiritual law during my second year at Muhlenberg. Instead of just saying Greek life wasn't for me and moving on, I wanted to change them—I wanted to take them down. I took my feelings right to the office of the president of the college. When we met, I was hit with some good news and bad news. The good—he agreed with me! We shared the same feelings on the institutionalized social exclusivity. The bad—his hands were tied. The alumni were funding the school—so my plan of abolishing Greek life from the entire campus was looking pretty grim. A girl can try.

When I lost the battle against the Greeks, I decided to transfer to Juniata College in Huntingdon, Pennsylvania. (Coincidently, that same summer, Muhlenberg's president "quit under fire" or was "ousted" depending on which newspaper you read. Go figure.) You might say my transferring colleges was the beginning of my nomadic years. You see, I didn't *actually* want to go to college in my hometown. My real reason for transferring to Juniata was to take part in their semester abroad program. So, my first semester as a Juniata student, I shipped off to the University of Gloucestershire in Cheltenham, England. That was when I learned an important thing about myself—when I'm abroad, I'm invincible. It's impossible for me to have a bad day in a foreign country—trust me, I've now tested this theory from Argentina to Sweden and many, many places in-between. As you can imagine, after spending a semester in my land of invincibility, I was feeling a bit reluctant to return to the States. This led to spring breaks and studying in Ireland, Northern Ireland, and Brussels, to name a few.

On one trip back from Ireland, the resistance I thought I'd left at Muhlenberg re-surfaced.

Thus far in life, my method for coping with the trials of college life had been planning for the next trip. I avoided dealing with the hurt and defeat I experienced the first two years of college by focusing on my next jaunt across the pond to Europe. The coping method of escape was no longer an option. I was required to finish my college career in the states. All of the heaviness I had been running from was now staring me right in the face. I was trying so hard to fight my way through instead of looking inward to find happiness.

It didn't take long for that negative mindset to begin manifesting in my physical body.

Cue health crisis.

Every single part of us is associated with a certain feeling or emotion—I can tell you from both study and first-hand experience that the gallbladder is connected with anger and resentment, and that's exactly what I felt when I returned from studying in Ireland over spring break. I could barely breathe, the pain in my chest was so intense I thought I was having a heart attack, and I was vomiting uncontrollably from said pain. My boyfriend and dad had to physically carry me down the steps of my apartment in order to bring me to my final diagnosis: Forty-two gallstones.

Interestingly, there was no medical explanation for my condition or the sudden onset of so many stones. I'd never had a day of indigestion. I was 20 years old. I was not overweight. I had no family history of gallstones.

I sure was carrying around some heavy emotions, though.

I'd spent my senior year of college missing England and the friends I'd met while abroad. Luckily, I had a new and wonderful reason for living. Her name was Bailey Lizabeth, and she was a beautiful and brilliant chocolate Lab, a.k.a. *my everything*. Bailey reminded me of my connection with Maggie and the role pets play in healing their humans. In a tip-of-the-iceberg kind of way, my ability to communicate with animals was poking me, asking, "Remember me?"

With the help of Bailey, finishing college became a tolerable task; with the help of a professor before I left Muhlenberg, I made another course adjustment in my career. She informed me that, although being a psychologist in the FBI might be my dream, I was more likely to land a life of talking to bored housewives, not serial killers. So, I replaced the psychology half of my double major with

Peace and Conflict Studies—another reason Juniata was a perfect fit because I could pursue this new area of study while traveling the world. Beyond college, it was off to my next step in life: law school.

Looking back, I don't think it's a coincidence I got the gallstone diagnosis the same week I was supposed to visit my first law school campus. Part of me believes that I was experiencing the universe's first attempt at telling me that practicing law wasn't for me. I didn't catch this intuitive hit back then, so instead of cancelling, we simply rescheduled our visit.

I almost went to Notre Dame but landlocked South Bend, Indiana, was so not happening after I visited Bristol, Rhode Island. My final school of choice was Roger Williams University in Rhode Island—picked solely on geography. I took Baily with me, of course. In fact I have to admit, life improved a lot while I was in law school. I had my dog and my very own, super cute apartment only a block from the water. It was my first time living without any other humans, and it was easily the happiest and healthiest I had ever been in my life.

It wasn't until I was halfway through law school that I started to feel resistance. Instead of listening to it and trying to understand it, I pushed through. I knew I didn't want to be a lawyer; I thought about doing non-profit work or maybe going into the Peace Corps. Still, I decided to finish law school and make the most of the time I had.

In the summers, when most law students were busy with summer associate positions at competitive law firms, I would jet off to Oxford University to study international human rights, London for a judicial clerkship at Harrow Crown Court, and Portugal to learn international cyber security laws. So we're clear, I was not interested in cyber law in the least, but I *was* very interested in Lisbon.

Knowing I didn't want to practice law in the traditional sense, I secretly vowed never to take the bar exam and planned to look for work in Washington, DC, when I graduated. My last year of law school took an interesting and unexpected turn, and a new route emerged: The path to Texas.

It started when I flew to Houston for a friend's wedding. That's where I met a curious young man who would soon become my new boyfriend, we'll call him C.

We had just finished up the rehearsal dinner and were making our way across a parking lot to the bar that would be housing the night's remaining debauchery. I looked over and saw some guy walking on top of the concrete tire stops like they were balancing beams.

Seriously? How old is this kid?

In the same mental breath, I heard intuitively: "You will grow old with him."

At first, I was perplexed. My logical mind jumped to judgement and thought he should be a little more mature, and yet, I felt a strong attraction to everything that made him so carefree. He was everything about my childhood that growing up, I'd made wrong.

We didn't have much contact for the rest of the trip, but as it turned out I had made quite the impression on him. Three weeks later, I was back in Rhode Island when I got a call from the bride.

"Hey, do you remember C from the wedding?"

I pondered for a moment. "Was he the one that looked like the lady on the logo for Chiquita® bananas? Or the one with the eyebrows?"

"Eyebrows," my friend replied. "He says he wants to fly up here to hang out with you, but he's going to pretend that he's here to see us."

"Wow, you really just blew his cover."

"Just play along, okay?"

I agreed to do just that. When C showed up, we ended up going out for a fun night at a casino with my friends.

When we were alone, he said, "I'm going to kiss you by the end of the night."

"Oh really?" I replied.

C was a lucky guy, but not that lucky. Although his prophesied kiss did come true, I sent him to bed in the spare room. The next morning, he informed me that during the night, he came to wake me up and talk a few times, but every time he approached my bedroom doorway, Bailey stood up and glared at him.

His visit came to a close, but we stayed in touch. Quickly, a relationship started to form.

There was a familiar energy and the whole relationship felt like déjà vu. Ours was a whirlwind and we were in each other's company as much as our schedules allowed, which required a lot of plane rides from Rhode Island to Texas and some exciting road trips, too. My last semester at RWU Law was like I wasn't even in law school anymore. Somewhere along the way I decided to bag my plans for DC and move to Houston, where C lived. If I was going to have to practice law, I wanted it to be immigration. H-town seemed like a no-brainer.

Before I knew it, I was sitting in a modern efficiency apartment with my law degree and whatever else I could squeeze in my car thinking, *Holy shit . . . I just moved to Texas. What am I thinking?*

But there wasn't much to think about; there was only fun to be had. I'd spent so much time traveling to Texas over the last couple of months that C's friends had become my friends too. Many of them lived in Galveston, at the beach.

Most nights were spent in friendly bars on the Gulf where everyone knows everyone else. There were also many trips to Hill Country to float the Guadalupe River and camp. Basically, I was feeding my soul in every way I could. The problem was, I also needed to be feeding my bank account.

So began the job hunt.

I tried sticking to my resolution of not taking the bar exam (and it worked for one year); I had absolutely no interest in becoming a traditional lawyer. The problem was, every job I applied for asked the same question, in so many words, "Why haven't you taken the bar? Are you afraid you'll fail?"

I get it. It's hard to look at something like that on someone's resume and understand that it's just a personal line in the sand they've drawn. So, after pressure from potential employers, I finally said, "fine," but on one condition. I was adamant (and told everyone) that if I took it and didn't pass the first time, then it was a sign from God that I'm never supposed to practice.

The Texas bar is a three-day exam. As far as I was concerned, it was a three-day test in being let off the hook of legal work.

Well, dammit.

I passed the exam on the first try.

Okay . . . I guess I'm a lawyer now . . . I have to practice . . .

When I set my mind to it, it didn't take long for me to get a job, and it didn't take long for *that* to interfere with the soul-feeding life I'd built in Texas. One step towards practicing law was one giant step away from the beach. Funny backstory, the day I mailed my bar application was the same day my friends and I got into a teeny tiny predicament with the Texas Alcoholic Beverage Commission for "drinking in a bar after hours"—the best part—I was in my pajamas and stone sober waiting for a friend to finish his shift. Sober or not, it was illegal for me to be in a bar with open containers after hours. Oh, the irony. I got in trouble with the law the same day that I applied to take the bar exam. That's a warning sign if I ever saw one, but what else was I supposed to do? Throw my law degree into the Gulf?

The next few years weren't too bad—ups and downs, work and play.

As part of the natural human aversion to sustained happiness, now that I had my degree, I started making trouble in other areas of my life. As my life's focus shifted towards law, my mind drifted away from ideas like fun at the beach, and so did my connection with C. I was facing up against the classic choice between love and money.

After my first day at work, C came over to my place to celebrate with a glass of wine or two. Just before bed, he went into the bathroom to brush his teeth and never came out, until I knocked to ask if he was okay.

He came out, sat down with me, and said, "I don't think I can do this."

"Do what?"

"You're not going to be able to play all day, pick me up from the airport, hang out on the beach." He shook his head. "You have a job now." After a moment's hesitation, he added. "I just wish I could put you on a shelf for ten years and take you off when I'm ready to settle down."

I wasn't insulted; I got it. His lifestyle and mine were starting to conflict. Still, I had to be honest. "I'm not the type of girl that you put on a shelf."

Things with C were on and off for about six months, but eventually, the time for fun and games was over. We realized we needed to pick one or the other: together or not.

Not.

Like I said, ups and downs.

I made some great new friends after C and I broke up. I moved into the heart of Houston, the museum district. A little over two years after moving to Texas, I met the man that would become my husband.

My friend had convinced me to sign up for an online dating account. By sheer luck, elsewhere in Houston, a man named Raul was under similar pressure from a friend of his own.

The first handful of guys I met didn't exactly make me feel compelled to keep up the search. Just before my account's free trial period came to an end, Raul found me and asked if I wanted to meet him for brunch at a place called Hugo's. By this point, I had burned out on meeting strangers from the internet, but my friend convinced me it would be worth it.

"Hugo's has the best brunch. You have to go, just for that."

Fair enough . . .

My friend was right; the brunch was great. As for my date? Let's just say that we were in for a long warm-up period. Raul was full of himself and as equally uninterested in a serious relationship as I was.

"So, you're online dating," I started. "What are you looking for?"

"A nice girl," he replied. "From a nice family. Well-educated." As he hit a few of the other generic points, I received an intuitive hit of what his next words were going to be.

I just want somebody who gets me . . . and no one is ever going to get me.

Raul said the first half, but stopped before the second came out. I knew then that in his mind he had created a Catch 22. He would settle for someone that understood him, but had already convinced himself that no one could ever fit that bill.

The first impressions we both gained on that first date weren't exactly flattering. I walked away from the whole encounter thinking, *Who the hell does he think he is? He's not all that and a bag of chips. Someone has to cut him down to size, and I'm the one to do it.*

He would later admit that he thought I dressed like a nun and put on a facade for the world. He only decided to keep seeing me because he thought I might have cute friends and said he knew there was more to me than the tough exterior.

With this attitude, we kept seeing each other about once a week. He was a completely different person from C.

Although Raul worked in the same industry as C (heck, by then so did I—it's Houston after all—who doesn't work in oil and gas?), he was the flip side of C in many ways. Raul was more into control and organization, rather than C's planless, listless drifting through life. Raul was a "grown up," not a guy that hung out in beach bars and played as hard as he worked. He preferred downtown and midtown bars. It was exciting; I had a whole new and different world to explore with this man.

The energy that brought Raul and I together was different from my past relationships. Before we met, we were both sad in our own ways. He was growing tired of traveling the world for work and was dealing with some pretty heavy stuff with his parents. For me, the luster of the city was starting to wear off and work was getting me down. I think we attracted each other because we were both miserable.

Our relationship continued to blossom in its own strange way, and eventually I mentioned him to my mom on the phone. My dad called me back the same day for a casual interrogation.

"So I hear you spent the night at some guy's place. What's going on? Is it serious?"

I laughed at that one. "Absolutely not. This guy has two other girlfriends in Dallas and one in Venezuela. This is literally just a social experiment to see if I can show him that he's not *'all that.'*"

Flash forward four days. Raul is in Bolivia on business. He calls me from his hotel room at 3AM.

"Hey . . . do you wanna get married?"

It was so out of nowhere that I thought he was just asking me my general opinion on the institution of marriage. "I'm not sure I would ever really get married."

"No. Do you want to marry me?"

Oh. That's what you mean?

"I don't know . . . " I started to say.

"It's a yes or no question. Do you want to get married?"

"Sure," I replied, though I didn't think either of us was being serious. My answer was more about calling his bluff than any kind of meaningful commitment.

Little did I know, he had already been in touch with my parents and gotten in touch with my favorite goldsmith to craft the perfect ring.

Growing up, my friend John Robert would occasionally call me "KGB," a nickname I earned for being extremely proficient in the art of espionage (and tattle-telling on him and his friends for smoking in the alley in junior high). So, while Raul was working behind the scenes with my parents to plan a proper proposal (as opposed to a late night international phone call), I was reading about all of it in my mother's email, which I had hacked the moment I got a whiff of a surprise.

As anticipated, Raul dropped to one knee and popped the question in December while I was home for Christmas.

He brought me to the private studio of my favorite goldsmith under the guise of simply ring shopping, but the perfect ring was already there waiting for me.

It was a gold band with platinum accents and a true old mine, cushion cut diamond, meaning no machinery was used in its creation. Its authenticity was of the utmost importance to Raul. It meant that it would look its best when held in candle light, as opposed to the modern cuts which are designed to shine in artificial light.

So, there in the home studio of James Meyer, a jeweler with creations in the Smithsonian, I became Raul's fiancée. After we made it official, we enjoyed a grand holiday engagement party with friends and family. At one point, a friend pulled me aside.

"You never even told us you were dating anyone and now you're suddenly engaged," she said, only a minor note of concern in her voice. "What's going on?"

"Oh, you know how I roll. We'll just see where it goes."

"Keveney. You're wearing a ring. Raul already reserved a church. This is happening."

She was right. Only one year later, Raul and I got married.

It may seem like getting married to this man was an odd choice, but I think love itself can be like that. Even though Raul and I got off to a rough start, he proved to me how hard he was willing to work to surprise me, to make me happy. I saw love in him, and that's exactly what caused me to say "yes."

From there, things started to slip. Back in Pennsylvania, my grandma's health was deteriorating. In Houston, I learned that Raul loved to drink more than I thought. At first, I thought it was just because we were in our honeymoon period, going out all the time and doing what new couples do. Slowly, I came to the realization that the drinking was more than that. When we cooled off with our nights out on the town, his drinking kept its usual pace at home. He didn't need bars or crazy nights out to get drunk—just a bottle and some free time. I'm not someone who has tolerance for drunk people, so you can imagine what it was like for me to be living with one. I knew he wasn't happy with his choices, either.

The air in our apartment was starting to feel dark and heavy. Raul's drinking increased and so did my weight. The energy around us was toxic, suffocating. Thankfully, we decided to get a dog for our one year wedding anniversary—enter Kaspi.

I can only imagine what it was like for her to step into the swamp-like energy. For me, she was a reason for being. She offered me both her love and a place to put my own. I think I did a great job keeping her happy despite the environment that I brought her into. It wasn't sustainable, of course, but Kaspi and I both put up a good fight against the darkness.

The hard times continued, and I found myself on the phone with Grandma more and more. She was my sounding board, the one who would let me vent—no strings attached. Everyone else I talked to about my problems wanted to offer advice. They would tell me what was good for me—what I should and shouldn't be worried about. Not Grandma Evelyn, though. I can remember once running out of a restaurant with tears in my eyes to get away from the "advice" that my mom and her friend were giving me. I know they only wanted to comfort me and couldn't stand to see me so sad. Still, I was inconsolable. I got into my car, dialed my grandma, and sobbed . . . and sobbed . . . and sobbed.

She didn't say a word.

The other end of the line was completely silent as she

listened. She was a natural healer and a crucial part of my existence. I wasn't sure how I could ever survive without her, but as it turned out I would have to learn soon. Some lessons take time. This one would take years.

CHAPTER 5
My Rock and My Light

❧

A LL THROUGH THOSE years of high school, college, law school, and life in Houston, my grandma was learning to live with some new health challenges. Many would have considered these to be major setbacks—however, Grandma Evelyn took them in stride and paid little attention to them for as long as she could. I truly don't think many people would have taken macular degeneration as gracefully as my grandma. Tiny blood vessels had formed in her eye and were leaking blood into her retina. It was only a matter of time before scars formed and completely obscured her vision. Back then, there weren't as many viable treatments for the condition as there are now, and to make things even more difficult—she had the worse of the two varieties (wet, not dry).

After being diagnosed, within the space of less than three years, Grandma went from having clear vision, driving wherever she wanted, and working as a beautician, to being legally blind. She accepted the condition and made it work for her just fine; she was determined to maintain her independence for as long as possible.

Macular degeneration only takes the center of your

vision, so Grandma retained some peripheral vision. Sometimes she would catch things out the side of her eye that the rest of us missed. On more than one occasion we'd be driving at night when she suddenly started shouting about a deer she had spotted on the side of the road. None of us ever saw those deer.

Despite being blind, she went right on living in her three-story Victorian home, alone, for years. She already knew where everything was—right down to how many steps were in the double wooden staircase that led upstairs. She wasn't going to move out of that place until she was good and ready (and found the perfect family willing to pay her price for the house, an amount she set based on exactly what she wanted and nothing else). All of us knew better than to argue with her.

The adversity she was facing didn't stop at macular degeneration. The inciting incident of her next setback was so long ago, but I remember it like it was yesterday.

One Christmas while we were visiting her, Grandma felt under the weather and a bit congested. Plus, her once new knee replacements were now almost two decades old. She had promised us she'd sleep downstairs on nights when she was feeling especially tired or achy. That night, she decided to take full advantage of the bed in the dining room and not make the journey upstairs.

My dad and "her girls" (as she lovingly referred to my mom, Aunt Karen, Whitney, and me) were sleeping upstairs when I heard a sound coming from the bottom of the staircase.

"Mom," I whispered, waking her. "Did you hear that?"

It sounded like Grandma calling us, and now it was gone. After a minute of silence, my mom insisted it was just a dream. The second time I woke up, I knew I wasn't just hearing my own thoughts. There was a faint gurgling, wheezing sound coming from downstairs. I heard Grandma weakly call out to us a second time. She was saying, "Girls, girls, girls," over and over again. I threw off the covers and ran downstairs.

Grandma had hobbled from the dining room across the kitchen and into the music room. She now stood doubled over the wooden column at the base of the staircase. She was struggling to breathe, let alone talk. My mom and aunt jumped into action; Mom grabbed the Vicks and began boiling water hoping a hot, eucalyptus steam might loosen things up. The truth could be seen right in my grand-mother's eyes.

"We need to call an ambulance," I said. My mother and aunt knew how much Grandma didn't like making a fuss or taking an unnecessary ambulance ride, so they were doing everything they could to try and make her comfortable at home. Within minutes, it was clear to all of us that the usual over-the-counter remedies were not going to work.

We looked at my grandma, who couldn't say "yes," but she nodded to us. That sealed the deal. She was not the biggest fan of doctors—so if she was saying it was time to call an ambulance, it was time. When we got to the hospital, the doctor told us how wise it had been for us to bring her in so quickly. This wasn't a case of allergies or a common head cold. Grandma Evelyn was suffering from congestive heart failure (CHF).

Grandma wasn't ready to check out just yet. Her immediate prayer was to see her granddaughters graduate high school; me in a few months and Whitney four years later.

Her condition improved enough that she continued living alone in that big house for several years. Of course, she was receiving regular visits from all of us, but she wasn't relying on anyone. When she was finally ready to leave, in her mind, it had nothing to do with her health—only logic.

"I don't need all of this space. What am I going to do with it?"

Even in the move, Grandma Evelyn was fiercely independent. She insisted on doing most of the packing on her own. Thus began the process of a blind woman sorting through a lifetime of belongings for a move from a three-story home into a small apartment. Her process was simple: She would pick up the first thing she touched, feel it, smell it, and shake it. If none of her other senses could tell her what the item was, she threw it in the trash assuming she "must not need it too badly."

Well before my time, she and my grandpa owned a general store. Her attic housed much of the memorabilia from those days, and we often wondered what antiques she likely ditched—old Coca-Cola signs, Barbie dolls, stuff that was probably worth a decent bit of money to the right collector. An auction might have yielded more than just some extra pocket money.

"Well it's not worth anything to me," Grandma replied. "It's just sitting in the attic collecting dust."

The move into her apartment was smooth and quick, considering she had taken her worldly possessions down to bare-bones (with the exception of her Christmas decorations which were nonnegotiables). Once there, she went right on living her independent lifestyle, only with less square footage to cover.

The CHF kept her going back-and-forth to the hospital for years. Her condition was slowly getting worse, and the episodes began happening more often. It was December 2009, a decade after the initial diagnosis, and things were looking quite grim; we thought we were going to lose her. Then, all of a sudden, she rallied and made it home just in time for Christmas (I think she was determined to make it home to check out Raul as it would be the first time I'd be bringing him home to Pennsylvania, and, as you've already learned, unbeknownst to me, he was planning to propose and had been organizing an engagement party with my mom for friends and family). Despite Grandma getting to come home for the holiday, we were scared. As hard as she tried, she wasn't her chipper self. We could see how much she'd declined, and the doctors told us there was not much else to do for the CHF. It was a foreboding step towards the end of her independence. The general mood of the family was centered around one wish—one last Christmas together with loved ones.

It was around this time when Grandma started putting the pieces together. Her congestion was normally at its worst around the holidays. There was no way this could be a coincidence. It all boiled down to one thing: This was the time of year that her eating habits were less than ideal—big meals, lots of snacks, ham, salty chex mix, and cookies. She wondered if this influx of sugar and salt had something to do with her congestion and the CHF episodes. She decided to begin measuring all her fluids so as not to exceed a certain daily allowance, and she'd give up the extra salt (cookies and fudge weren't going anywhere). The doctors agreed that it was worth a shot, and it turned out to be worth way more than that.

From that Christmas onward, my grandmother measured absolutely everything. Soup broth, Jell-O, juice—she sorted all of it out with measuring cups. Her plan worked like a charm and her congestion returned to manageable levels.

"I'm not ready to die, I'm not going to miss out on all the fun you girls are having." She said these words often, and she was right. Instead of just seeing one more Christmas, Grandma Evelyn saw a total of five more, and not only was she at my high school graduation and Whitney's, she attended all of our ceremonies—college and law school for me, and college and a Master's for Whitney. She'd even live to see my wedding day. Truth be told, I think she surprised herself; I know she surprised all of us. We'd almost lost her so many times over the last 14 years, it was like she'd become immortal—none of us were prepared for the end.

The final year of her life, she was in and out of the hospital almost monthly. Since her body was no longer producing red blood cells, she'd also been getting Procrit injections, a man-made protein that helps the body do what hers was no longer able to do.

Of all the ways to lose her, she almost died from an uncontrollable nosebleed, which required an emergency transport to a major hospital before it could be stopped.

Still fighting. Still living. Still smiling.

As brave as she was, my grandmother was starting to fear her own death. I think that's pretty reasonable. Like she said, she didn't know what happens after we die. She didn't think this was the last stop, though, and the unknown can be a pretty ominous thing. My mom and aunt would spend as much time in the hospital with her as they could.

She and I were on the phone constantly. It says a lot about her that despite all of her medical issues, she was usually the one listening to me complain. She had this incredible way of drawing pain from me.

On one of our calls, she told me about a dream she had that was equal parts interesting and upsetting. She was at a huge party and everyone she knew and loved was there, except for "her girls." In the dream, right around the time she noticed her girls were missing, she realized something else. Everyone at the party had already passed on.

As my grandmother put it to me on the phone, she thought, "Awe hell, I'm not going to *that* party. They're all dead, and my girls aren't here!" She turned away from the dream and walked back into the waking world to be with her girls. She told the story with a constant laugh in her voice, but that dream definitely altered her thinking. I know that I believe she had almost crossed over that night, and I think she believed that, too. From that day forward, there was a fear in her that I'd never before seen.

We all thought that she would be drifting away from us before she made it out of the hospital. The dream just seemed like a sign of what was coming. She was a fighter, though, and she ended up coming home again.

"Home" by now was actually my aunt's home. Grandma had finally given up her independent lifestyle in her apartment. I think we all breathed a sigh of relief when she agreed to that one, including her. It was difficult for me to be living so far away from her during all of these troubles she was having. I took frequent flights back and forth to see her, but there's only so much I could do "working for the man" in corporate America.

Soon after arriving home, we learned that Grandma caught *C. diff*, a bacterial infection, at the hospital. Plus, her kidneys were beginning to fail.

But she was still fighting, still laughing.

On Thursday, April 3, 2014, my mother called to tell me Grandma's infection was not improving, and her health was failing quickly. My aunt and mom were talking to hospice and deciding whether to bring in a hospital bed now or wait until Monday. It was a question of soon or sooner.

By Friday, we had all decided right now would be best.

While hospice was there on Friday afternoon, my Grandma had another bout of congestion—or perhaps a panic attack realizing that this time *was* different than all the others. We didn't know how much time she'd have left, but we figured it was a matter of weeks. In typical Grandma fashion, she turned the fight around and was up and perky the next morning.

"Those darn doctors are wrong again! I'm gonna beat this. Where's my coffee? Get me out of bed. I can't sit around looking like this."

Not that she was a woman who needed much caffeine to keep her going.

My aunt went off to work that Saturday morning, and Mom helped Grandma change into a clean, white nighty with tiny pink flowers and a pink and white Gingham housecoat—both of which still hang in my closet. Mom also gave her a manicure while she drank her coffee.

It made me so happy to hear her talking like that. Every time she had one of these rebounds, I felt a burst of positive energy. I had a great convo with her that morning—we laughed, and we cried. In what almost seemed like parting advice, she made me promise never to let a man make any decisions for me. We all went to bed Saturday evening breathing a sigh of relief—little did we know, she wouldn't get out of bed again.

By Sunday morning, her kidneys were really failing . . . and they didn't seem to be wasting any time. I talked to Mom Sunday afternoon, and she said I might want to think about flying home later in the week. Hospice estimated Grandma had only about a week or two until her body would quit for good.

Sunday night I woke up suddenly from a deep sleep— 3:33 AM. Monday morning to be exact. Ringing in my ears repeatedly were the words, "Get a ticket now. Go home now. NOW." I knew with every cell of my being it was time.

How fast could I get there?

What was the earliest flight?

Would anyone even be able to pick me up from the airport? Hmm, my cousin Whitney would have to.

I ran into the living room and grabbed my laptop. Raul woke up wondering what in the world I was doing bringing my computer to bed at almost 4 AM. I booked the earliest ticket I could find from Houston to Pittsburgh, where Whitney lived.

I waited until around 7 AM to call Mom to tell her the plan.

"I'm flying into Pittsburgh tomorrow. Whitney will have to pick me up from the airport."

"I don't know if Whitney can do th—"

"Whitney doesn't have a choice. This is what's happening."

On one hand, my mother *knew* this is what was needed to happen for Grandma to have all her girls together one last time. On the other hand, she tried calming me down, "I think you still have a couple more days. Don't panic. Don't rush."

"No, Mom. This is happening."

The following morning, Tuesday, April 8, 2014, Whitney did indeed pick me up from Pittsburgh airport, and we embarked on the 274-mile mad dash to Grandma, nestled in the mountains in northeastern Pennsylvania. There was no convenient airport so it made sense to hitch a ride with Whit. We stopped only once . . . to deal with the speeding ticket Whitney got along the way.

My mother told me whenever anyone would come in the house that day, Grandma would ask, "Keveney? Keveney? Is that Keveney?"

"No, she's coming. They're on their way," my mother replied, every time.

We pulled up to the house around 7 PM, and my

grandma had gone from occasionally being able to talk and joke around to no longer speaking. Her condition had deteriorated much faster than anyone had expected. I was so glad I hadn't waited to buy my ticket.

She could nod, giggle, and answer in hums—"mm hm," and "mm mm."

She would squeeze our hands to show that she was still aware of our presence.

My mother and I decided to take turns being alone with her, and since Mom had already been up for too many hours, I decided to take the first turn while she went to catch some rest on the couch.

After a few hours, I noticed that whenever my mother was in the room, Grandma would be calm and listen to her talk. Whenever I was alone in the room, she clearly wanted to say something. She was struggling to talk and even getting a little frustrated. I can only imagine that she wanted to give me some final advice—likely more about maintaining my independent spirit (ahem, stubbornness) and never sacrificing my dreams for a man—and felt like she hadn't gotten to say a proper goodbye.

Hospice told us to be on the lookout for what they call the "death rattle." It's the oddly dry and shaky sound of a baby rattle that comes from the back of the throat with every breath and usually signals that the end is near. I started to hear it and knew that we had reached the final hours of her life.

She would take what sounded like her final gasp of air, ten seconds or more would go by, and she would gasp again. It seemed that even then, she got a kick out of keeping us on our toes.

Around 4 AM, I called my mom into the room as Grandma seemed to be getting more and more agitated trying to talk to me. Mom began talking to her, promising to take care of her girls, and reciting the Lord's Prayer. I was on one side holding her hand and Mom on the other.

The room was suddenly bathed in a sense of peace, harmony, and order. Even though the only light in the room was coming from a nightlight, a kind of golden glow seemed to bloom all around me. My grandma went from looking sick and pained to being her old self again. Her smile turned up, she relaxed, and her breathing became nice and easy—a slow rise and fall of her chest.

The line between seeing and knowing blurred in that moment, and my mind could see the energy leaving her body. It looked, or felt, like particles of golden dust caught in the light of an old movie projector. She went from being in her body to suddenly filling the room and being all around us. It was honestly breathtaking and probably the most peaceful feeling I have ever experienced. It wasn't clinical death, not yet, but something more beautiful.

I suddenly understood that we're here on Earth for a much greater purpose than simply "kicking the can" (as Grandma would often say) or living to work and going through life feeling miserable. The suffering and pain that so many humans go through is not natural, and it's not what we're here to experience. This was one of the first and loudest times the Universe spoke directly to me as an adult.

The Universe was trying to tell me that something in my life needed to change. I needed to make an adjustment so that I could fulfill this greater purpose. It was an urging that I would resist right up until the night of Kaspi's seizure.

After seeing the light release from Grandma's body, I knew. Although her lungs were still breathing and her heart was still beating, she wasn't with us anymore. To me, my grandma's time of death was around 4:30 AM on the morning of April 9th. After that, I was okay with leaving the room to go lie down. It was like I had already said goodbye.

Mom stayed in the room and only laid her head down on Grandma's bed for a few minutes around 5:45 AM when she could no longer resist her heavy eyelids.

Mom and I woke up a few minutes after 6 AM when my mom's cousin, Robin, stopped for coffee on her way to work. Robin was a licensed practical nurse. She took one look at Grandma and tears filled her eyes.

"She's gone."

There's that old saying that people will wait until you leave the room or fall asleep to die. To most people who were there that day, that might seem true. To me, I knew that she had left us when Mom and I were by her side.

It gave me comfort to know that it wasn't really my grandma in that "box." She was no longer in her carbon-based shell. Really, there was nothing in that casket at all. The strong and independent woman that was such a big part of my life had already moved on to the next leg of her journey.

While we made funeral arrangements, we all stayed at my aunt's house; Raul, my dad, and Bailey (my chocolate Lab from college that became my dad's girl after I moved to Texas) had now joined Grandma's girls. The night before her funeral, I woke up in the middle of the night to the sound of Grandma's walker going across the floor. The human part of me simply thought that it was just a weird force of memory. When Grandma Evelyn was alive, she got up and moved to the bathroom with the help of her walker every night. My mind must have been calling up a familiar sound that wasn't actually there.

I went back to sleep only to wake up some hours later and see Grandma Evelyn at the foot of my bed, watching Raul and me sleep.

It's just a dream, right?

Not so.

The next morning over breakfast, Raul looked at me and asked if anything interesting happened last night. The memory of what I saw was hazy enough that I had to ask him what he was talking about.

"Your grandma was totally at the foot of our bed last night watching us sleep. It was really freaky."

I had always known that Raul had his own unique ability to sense things in his surroundings that are not of this Earth. Unlike my abilities, his were closed off from years of seeing primarily darkness. This was one of the first times that his gift was active as an adult, because of the sheer abundance of love, safety, and security that my grandma brought with her.

Experiences like that tend to soften terms like "the loss of my grandmother." It's hard for me to believe that anyone is really completely lost when I know that there is an energetic part of them still drifting around, somewhere between the air that we breathe and the places in the universe that we won't understand until it's our time to go. We are made of energy, and energy *cannot* be destroyed—we *must* go somewhere.

So that said, now you know how I "lost" the one person that I could go to who would just listen. She was the one that could make any obstacle seem easy to surmount, any confusing situation seem simple. She is still with me in a few ways. Aside from the occasional presence of her energy, many of her words stayed with me too.

"You can wake up in the morning and complain about your aches and pains," she would say, "Or you can think 'This is great. I can still put one foot in front of the other and that's exactly what I'm going to do.'"

I called upon those words on more than a few mornings during my legal career.

Even with her positive energy still with me, I no longer had my sounding board. Without that voice on the other end of the phone, a crucial vent of my frustration had closed off. The negative energy was trapped in me with no place to go other than my home, my marriage, and my dog—Kaspi. This would be the beginning of the two most difficult years in my life, which led straight to the crisis with Kaspi. The final years before her seizure are what I refer to as "The Lost Years." It's an appropriate title, as you're about to see.

CHAPTER 6
The Lost Years

❧

I WASN'T LIVING; I was going through the motions. The years immediately following my grandma's death were beyond challenging. I felt like I was floating somewhere above my body looking down on myself—like I was seeing my life go by almost as if I was watching a bad movie. Empty spaces in my memory started cropping up all over the place. There were events and parties that I was physically present at and then had no recollection of them. A trailer for a movie would come on TV, and I'd express interest in seeing it only to have Raul remind me that we'd seen it weeks ago.

I often refer to this phenomenon as "popping out of my body." During the lost years, my physical body was in this world. In another way, though, I was off in a completely different place and space.

My legal career spanned a decade. It began at a national Equal Employment Opportunity (EEO) compliance firm and ended at a Professional Employer Organization (PEO)—with immigration cases (which I loved) and oil and gas discovery law (which I hated) peppered in between. As far as "working for the man" is concerned, I saw some of the worst of the worst. I'd wrestled with the difference between my romantic career ideals to change the world compared with the reality of my day job from the day I graduated law school. The only difference between then and now was that I no longer had my grandma to help me through the struggles and offer light in the darkness.

The walls closed in on me. I felt surrounded by male chauvinists and the women that supported them (both inside and outside the workplace), unethical behavior, and hate. Conversations went something like this . . .

"A Mexican husband, huh?"

"That's right," I replied.

"I never thought you were the type."

"And what type is that?"

"Ah," he waved off my question. "He's got an Ivy League education. Pretty surprising for a Mexican, so I guess that makes him okay."

(Never mind Raul was born and raised in Texas.)

Several ladies in the office sat me down and told me things like, "Honey, you're not in the North anymore. This is the South. You're here to look pretty. You're here to get them coffee." Then came the worst part. "Here, you say 'yes, sir'." I wondered, is this 1950 or 2015?

Women I met outside of work judged me for wanting a career while pitying me for not having any children. They also looked down on my husband for "making me work." These perceptions couldn't have been farther from the truth.

My reaction to this was less than desirable. Without my grandma, my sounding board and my optimist, I became extremely resistant and judgmental. I was frustrated with the good ole boy bosses that looked down on me because I married a Hispanic man and made me (and my husband) feel wrong for wanting a seat at their table. I was frustrated with the women that worked beside me and seemed okay taking a backseat to their male counterparts. I judged the women who didn't have an education or weren't in control of their money. I became obsessed with making everyone else wrong, and I decided that all Texans were the same and were to blame for my experiences and troubles. I was still a long way from recognizing my own negative judgements, and my daily chatter went something like this:

All Texans are racist, backward, and uneducated. How could they be so naive? How could they live in this White man's world and be okay with it?

The lost years tested me. Maybe it's worth invoking the old phrase, "forged in flames." The flames were definitely high during these times. My marriage was on the brink of total failure. Raul's drinking was at its worst. There were countless variables at play in this decline. One of the heaviest forces pulling me down was the dark energy that had inhabited our house, long before we moved in. We were not alone in that building—we'd never been alone. We purchased our house in 2012; I thought back to our buying experience and started to connect the dots.

We had picked a great realtor who did everything she could to make the process an easy and enjoyable one. She showed us many houses, but Raul had hang-ups about each one. Something just wasn't fitting his preferences . . . until the one we ended up buying.

I loved the neighborhood and the floor plan, but something about the house itself was very off-putting to me. The Universe itself tried telling us not to move into the place by getting us stuck in option pending for *way* too long. The resistance was all around us, but for some reason, we kept pushing through; Raul was determined that this was *the* house.

Right after we closed on the house, I took my friend, Beth, and Kaspi to check it out. When we parked outside,

Beth had a funny look. It was as if she was saying, "Really? This house?"

She wasn't commenting on the aesthetics of the place. Everyone liked the curbside appeal; Beth was picking up on the energy the house was letting off—not good. Her reaction was real and visceral.

Once we got inside the house, she looked to a corner by the front door and didn't take her eyes off it. Beth was from Louisiana and had her fair share of supernatural experiences. "I will not stand with my back to that corner. Ever."

"What do you see?" I asked.

"I'm not going to talk about anything specific, but I'm telling you right now . . . I'm not turning my back on it."

We went through the rest of the house with Kaspi staying close by. When we arrived at the end of the hallway and stepped toward the master bedroom, Kaspi's pace slowed and her hair started standing up. By the time we were in the master bedroom, she looked incredibly uncomfortable. After glancing into the master bathroom just for a second, she seemed to transform from docile Labrador to Rottweiler. Teeth showing, hair up, growling at nothing.

Beth and I didn't see something the way I believe Kaspi did, but we definitely felt a heavy and unsettling energy. Beth said, "Okay . . . I'm not going in there either. You need to get some sage, diffuse some Palo Santo, have a priest come, do all the things to clear this place."

After we were fully moved in, we got to know our neighbors quickly. Our immediate neighbors were beyond excited to see the former owner go. The common response after pointing our new house out was, "Oh, I'm so glad he doesn't live here anymore."

From then on, neighbors started to come out of the woodwork with stories . . .

The previous owner was a school teacher and coach that got fired for stealing from the school.

He was addicted to drugs.

His dealers came by in the middle of the night and stole his car.

He made money by offering to paint people's houses, but would only work two hours before walking off and never finishing the job.

One night, he woke everyone in the neighborhood up as he threw his wife's belongings and antique furniture out into the street.

We didn't know which, if any, of these stories were exactly true. Yet, all of these things helped explain why Raul was so attracted to the house. He was struggling with drinking of his own and coping with a tremendous amount of anger over some issues with his family. This, combined with my own disgust over my career, turned us both into negativity magnets. The house couldn't resist us, and vice versa.

It wasn't just the energy in the house, though. My husband was in a frustrating place, too. He was working in corporate finance for an international oil and gas company, and it was getting him down. His company had been through a number of failed mergers, which meant he was in a constant state of re-interviewing for his job. Although Raul felt secure in his job, he was on a salary freeze and many of his friends and colleagues had been laid off. Needless to say, going to work during this time wasn't a pleasant experience for him.

He became more dissatisfied and, in turn, drank more often. Raul was an argumentative drunk—just two beers, and he'd be ready to disagree and fight all night. More often than not, he'd pick a fight with me about something stupid (like how many beers he'd drunk despite the evidence of the empty bottles). Often, I'd invite my lawyer friends over, hoping they'd distract Raul by arguing about politics or religion—anything to give me a break from his troubles.

On weekends, I'd sometimes put the dogs in the car and drive around for the sake of getting out of the house. I spent a lot of time at coffee shops and yoga studios, surviving by creating quiet spaces that I could retreat to. It got to the point where I didn't want to connect with any humans anymore. Sure, I had my girlfriends from home that I would talk to every day, but in terms of fellow Texans . . . no, thank you.

So, marriage and work troubles, what's left? My health again. In the years between my grandma's death and the wakeup call I received from Kaspi's seizure, my health took an absolute nose dive. My weight almost doubled. My hair began to fall out. I was always irritable. A trip to the doctor's office offered a few explanations for all of this. Diagnoses included hypothyroidism and adrenal failure. My cortisol levels were off the charts. After multiple efforts to take thyroid medication—synthetic, compounded, homeopathic, the list goes on—doctors determined medication wasn't an option for me because my body couldn't process it. My blood pressure spiked after a few weeks on each prescription. Imagine my frustration, being told what was wrong but there was nothing I could do about it. Actually, even then, I wasn't shocked that this was the reality; I've always been resistant to Western medicine and pharmaceuticals in general and wasn't the least surprised when they didn't work for me (no doubt I was clinging to my need to be right in this situation).

Around the time that my physical health was declining, I also stepped into the worst financial year of my life. I broke away from oil and gas (briefly) and ended up ping-ponging between a ton of different gigs. Jobs ranged from working as a staff attorney at a nonprofit and drafting anti-human trafficking legislation to consulting at my yoga studio. By the end of that year, I think I accrued six or seven W-2s and 1099s only to make less than half of what I made the previous year, a quarter of what my husband was pulling in.

All of that money and then some was funneled right back into Western medicine and holistic treatments for my various health issues. Despite my diagnosis, I actually felt okay (with the exception of shame over the almost 100 pounds I'd gained and anger for Texas). Each doctor had a different trick, and all of them were amazed at how I managed to work and exercise and be doing as well as I was, given my physical markers. My doctor prescribed a three-week veggie juice cleanse in an attempt to mitigate the issues. By the end of the three weeks, I had lost zero pounds. My gynecologist believed a 500-calorie restrictive diet and hormone injections would do the trick; I lost two pounds in fourteen days. Nothing was adding up. Everything I threw at my failing health seemed to be bouncing right back at me. Clearly, there was something more than physical illness that was causing all of this. When my gynecologist suggested another round of injections, I drew a line in the sand. Enough was enough. No more. I didn't know what was the answer, but I knew what I'd been doing wasn't it.

I had so many things pushing me to make a change in my life, and, in late 2014, I thought I'd found it. A friend introduced me to a man we'll call Jay. He seemed kind enough for a good ole White boy (an assessment I would later grow beyond and realize was just a facet of me being in total judgement). Jay was very interested in hiring me to help with his company. He needed an HR director and believed my experience in employment law was a great asset. I thought this was my ticket out of law. At times, it sounded too good to be true, but I convinced myself that my luck was about to turn and maybe this was grandma throwing me a Hail Mary (after all, Jay wasn't even from Texas originally).

Unfortunately, I had misread the entire situation. The

job morphed soon after I was hired. Suddenly, I found myself also being pulled into corporate compliance and asked to perform functions that should be reserved for in-house counsel (which his company failed to employ). For many reasons, I soon lost all respect for Jay. He was asking me to submit false information on official documents and commit fraud. Obviously I refused, but I began to fear for my law license which I'd kept active. Even if I didn't want to practice, I wanted it to stay in good standing.

I was drowning.

We've all heard the phrase "to every action there is an equal yet opposite reaction." I think my opposite reaction to my job was leaving Texas for a trip to Costa Rica. All throughout this transition to the new job, I had somehow managed to keep up practicing Bikram Yoga at my local studio. There were always posters up that advertised some kind of Bikram retreat. I never paid much attention to them before. Although I was feeling a slight nudge in the direction of becoming a yoga instructor, I didn't think I was physically or financially ready to spend tens of thousands of dollars to take the required courses for certification. Still, the push in that general direction was there . . . what was it *really* saying though?

Lucky for me, my grandma decided to pay me a visit during one of my classes and clear up the confusion. I couldn't see her walk in the door or anything like that. It wasn't a vision, but I could suddenly feel her all around me. She was in my energy field. Normally I would feel my absolute best when walking out of a yoga class. That day, I felt particularly wonderful. The moment I walked out the door, I noticed a brand-new poster for an all-women's Bikram retreat deep in the rainforests of Costa Rica.

That's what my grandma was pushing me towards. I knew then and there that she wanted me to go to Costa

Rica. I wasn't certain what I would find there, but I knew it was the next step that I needed to take. We'd practice Bikram two to three times a day—three to four-and-a-half hours of Bikram daily. The yoga aspect alone sounded great, and there was one other thing that was drawing me there: I simply wanted to get away and needed a change of scenery. I wanted to escape the concrete city and "be" in nature, and, thanks to my grandma, I had every reason to buy that ticket.

She hadn't steered me wrong. The trip was outstanding, and it gave my grandma another avenue through which she could offer guidance. As one might expect of a retreat like this, I was doing a great deal of soul searching while I was there. The idea of getting out of law and into something intuitive or healing-related was becoming a very attractive option, but I continued to resist it. Even if I decided to follow my instincts, I had no idea how to make a change like that. Once again, I soon received a gentle and blissful nudge in the right direction.

I caught some free time between the second and third hot yoga session of the day and decided to spend it in the delightful experience of sound healing and massage. As the singing bowls let out their soothing sounds, the visions started to flood my consciousness. I saw my entire life up until this point play out as if it was a movie. All during the show, I received what I can only describe as a total knowing. The gist of this intuitive download was that I must stop trying to make law fit my life. I was meant to do something else, something more intuitive, something that involved animals, something that allowed me to heal myself and others.

My grandma confirmed this sentiment. After the session ended, I stepped out into the rainforest and all of its green glory to see that something wonderful had been added to the scenery. There were pale yellow butterflies—too many to count—fluttering all around me. In the center of the dancing butterflies was a beautiful, tropical yellow flower. My grandma always loved yellow roses, and although I never saw a yellow rose in the rainforest, I knew for certain that this was my grandma's way of saying, "Yes." Yes to allowing myself to move forward without the need to force my law degree to fit.

It was the most valuable guidance I would take home from the retreat, and the beginning of the end of The Lost Years. For the first time since my grandma left this Earth, I had hope. In the following weeks, I began to intuitively understand how my thinking about Texas and corporate America contributed to my experience; I was in resistance and judgment and it was unnatural, bitter, and unproductive. I recognized that I was the problem—I was the common denominator in all of my experiences—and I started to take responsibility for how and why I pulled in other humans as miserable as me. It was the first time I considered that Texas might not be to blame and that I could shift perceptions about people from the South. The Truth was beginning to reveal itself.

CHAPTER 7
Remembering the Gift

...AND NOW WE'RE caught up to the night of Kaspi's seizure.

This would be the night I surrendered.

It was almost 5 AM by the time the vet came out into the waiting room and invited us to a private room. I hoped we would be seeing Kaspi, but that wasn't the case. They were only giving us an update on her condition. The vet had put her on a large dose of phenobarbital, essentially knocking her out to stop the seizures. It's the same substance they often use in higher doses to put animals to sleep. It's also used to treat humans with epilepsy, and it seemed they had found the right dosage to sedate Kaspi and ease the seizures. Although she was still seizing on a smaller scale, our girl seemed to be past the massive seizures she had in the wee hours of the morning.

Trying to get to the bottom of what was happening, the vet asked how old Kaspi was. The trouble was, we weren't certain. She was a rescue without a clear paper trail that led back to her birth. From the records we had and the condition of her teeth, we estimated she was about eleven. As it turned out, even if we were off a few years, it wouldn't make a difference. At Kaspi's age, there was no way this was epilepsy, and it certainly wasn't a random fluke. More likely than not, we were dealing with a blood clot, aneurysm, or brain tumor. Although they couldn't say for sure what it was, something in her brain had burst that night.

That was enough to confirm the intuitive download I had been sorting through since my frantic drive to the ER. Blood clot, tumor, whatever it was, it lined up perfectly with my belief that her brain was unable to process my stress. The negative energy of the household had made it into her with nowhere to go. Whether physical or metaphysical, build-ups like that can only lead to one thing: an explosion.

In order for us to know anything more, a scan would be necessary but neither the ER nor our regular vet had the capacity to administer one. We would have to go to a specialist. To make matters worse, we couldn't see a specialist before getting a referral from our vet. Though annoying, visiting our regular vet did seem like the best step forward. The ER doctors presented us with a few options, but strongly pushed for one in particular: euthanasia.

I firmly disagreed.

I told them I knew it wasn't a brain tumor—it simply wasn't.

My ability to pick up on the energy of people and pets was like my own form of x-ray vision. It was so finely tuned that I was even once able to pinpoint an exact diagnosis for my friend's dog before they took him in for an ultrasound. It's hard to deny that I have some ability to see under the fur when I could tell a friend that I saw congested energy around their dog's heart and spots on his pancreas and liver, only for the vet's ultrasound to come back hours later showing an enlarged heart and tumors on the pancreas and liver. With that and many other similar occurrences, I had come to really trust this ability.

Right now, the feeling it was giving me was stronger than ever. This couldn't be blamed on a tumor or physiological malady. This was my fault. Of course I sounded strange; it was a trait I would get used to people seeing in me over the coming years.

It was about 5:30 AM at this point—time for us to figure out our next move. Raul had a major meeting at work that day and had to make the hour-and-a-half journey across Houston soon in order to shower and make it to work on time. Plus, our regular vet didn't open for another hour and a half. Taking our sick dog away from the ER just to avoid rush hour traffic seemed wrong, so I made the decision that I would be doing *a lot* of driving that day.

Raul and I left the ER—without even being able to see Kaspi—so that I could get him home just in time for him to leave for work. Then came the rather brutal stretch of time where I was between vets and without the comfort of having Kaspi nearby. Well, I wasn't completely alone. Kinley was there, loving on me and comforting me in a way only she can do. I couldn't help but think of how lucky it was that she wasn't suffering from any kind of energetic malady like Kaspi was. We had gotten her toward the end of the Lost Years, which saved her from the bulk of the heavy energy that Kaspi had absorbed. We both helped calm each other down while I was home; she was sure glad to see me, but she was searching for Kaspi.

When it was finally time, I got in the car and buckled up for the haul back to the ER. I called our regular vet right when they opened at 7 AM, told them the situation, and warned them that we would be coming in. After a minor tussle with the beginnings of Houston's morning traffic, I pulled up to the ER. The techs were already there waiting to help me load her into the car.

"What do I need to know?" I asked. "What if she starts seizing again?"

The vet shook his head. "She's been completely stable, hasn't had one in a few hours. Given such high doses of phenobarbital she probably won't even wake up."

"Okay," I said, waited, then repeated, "But what happens if she starts seizing?"

His answer made me feel completely powerless. "Honestly, if she starts having a seizure there's nothing you can do. So, just keep driving."

It was surreal to see my lovely dog so completely checked out, almost gone from this realm. If I didn't know better, I would have thought she was dead. The residual stiffness from her seizure had faded away; she had become a ragdoll. Even though she was heavy and awkward to carry, Kaspi made it into my back seat and soon we were on our way.

Enter total gridlock.

If Kaspi had another massive seizure, I knew I wanted it to happen at the vet, not in the back of my car. That meant getting there fast, but speeding was no longer an option. I took a calming breath, got off the highway as soon as I could, and let myself follow whichever route my intuition told me to take. Letting go of control in that fashion was a great relief—I knew perfectly well that I would be guided to the vet in the most efficient route possible.

When I was about half way there, I was hit by a moment of total love and clarity. It was so sudden and so intense that tears began to fill my eyes. I could smell the intense fragrance of a very specific perfume—Elizabeth Taylor, White Diamonds. I certainly never owned or wore that particular perfume, but I knew someone who had. With that sudden breath of peace and understanding, I knew that my grandma was by my side, ready to help me through the day.

I had been burying myself in so much thought that morning—Raul, traffic, Kaspi, Kinley alone at home, and how I was going to completely overhaul my life—that I was getting overwhelmed. The download I received from Grandma seemed to simplify everything. Now wasn't the time to solve every problem at once. From this day and for the next eight months, I would have to take things minute by minute.

This was going to be a long process, not an overnight "ah-ha" moment. If I slowed my thinking and tackled problems as they came, I would be fine. The only other crucial thing for me to do? *Follow the guidance of my intuition.* The time for resisting the various calls I had been receiving was over.

My concern was becoming so powerful that I found myself preparing for the worst-case scenario. I can remember thinking to my Grandma, "If Kaspi can't come home with us and have a good quality of life, please just help her pass. Just let her fall asleep peacefully and not wake up."

Thoughts like that were enough to put my mind on the knife's edge of functioning. Much of that ride turned into lost time, much like the popping out of my body that was all-too-common during the lost years. I clearly remember the technicians loading Kaspi into the car, getting on the highway, and the visit from my grandma. Beyond that, I'm not sure where the memories went or what happened. I found myself pulling into the vet's parking lot soon after. I called them before I even put the car in park.

The team of techs they had standing by rushed out to meet me and took Kaspi into their care. Once again, I found myself in a waiting room with nothing but my thoughts. During that time I kept hearing, in the intuitive sense, "Just take her home and do what you did when you were a kid."

I'm not sure where those words came from and for a

while they only confused me. They were stronger than the consistent, chattering, internal monologue that we all have running in our heads at all times. My chatter had been going on overdrive that whole morning, thinking about things that were out of my control like what the vet was going to say, if Raul was going to get to work, and the fact that I was still wearing my pajamas in public.

This voice was different. It was so clear and present, as if a channel had opened up, cutting through the haze of thoughts to calmly, slowly deliver its message over and over.

"Just take her home and do what you did when you were a kid."

When I was a kid?

Mud potions and flower heists?

Then I remembered my games with Maggie. We didn't just play, we communicated on a deeper level. I thought back to our little game where I would send her pictures with my mind, and she would respond by either approaching one group of toys or another.

That must have been what Kaspi needed—love, attention, and communication. She needed a release for all of the dark energy she had absorbed over the years.

Like a mirror image to my trip to the ER, the vet emerged and brought me back into a room with Kaspi nowhere in sight. She gave me roughly the same diagnosis, only with a little more detail.

"Generally, when a dog has a seizure, it's one of three things," she said. "Epilepsy, some kind of tumor or blood clot, or brain cancer. Epilepsy usually shows up in young dogs, so since Kaspi is eleven years old we can rule that one out."

I barely felt relief, knowing that epilepsy was only one down, two to go.

"Given that she has no prior history of seizures, we're most likely looking at a blood clot she's had for a long time that finally ruptured."

I gulped. "And what about cancer?"

"There's no way to tell without a scan, but if it is cancer, Kaspi isn't a good candidate for chemotherapy because of her age. And if it's the blood clot . . . I'm sorry to say that those are typically terminal."

I knew what she was suggesting, but had to ask. "Are you saying we should put her to sleep?"

"That's up to you. All that I can say is that it might be the most peaceful option."

"Well, I'm not putting her to sleep," I said. "What other options do I have?"

The vet hesitated. "I could refer you to a specialist for a brain scan. That way, you might at least know what's causing the seizures, but knowing the cause wouldn't change the outcome. Whether it's a tumor or clot, your best bet will be to give Kaspi heavy doses of phenobarbital for the rest of her life."

I wrote off the brain scan.

I kept hearing, *No, it's not necessary. Take her home–today.*

I told our vet what I planned to do.

She gave me a warning. "It's extremely uncommon for an older dog to have an attack like this come on so suddenly. When something like this happens, you can almost be certain that more are coming in the near-future."

Most likely, this was not the end of Kaspi's seizures, and it might be best if I simply put her to sleep. It didn't take an intuitive download for me to know I wouldn't be going that route.

Lastly, the vet explained that I could keep her on a very low dose of phenobarbital in the hopes that it would suppress any future seizures. It would be a risky path with no guarantees, but to me it was the only way. When I told them I wanted to take Kaspi home, they agreed that I could take her home for a week or two and see how she managed. Looking back, I think what they were really trying to tell me was, "Take her home, spend some quality time with her, and be prepared to come back and put her down in about two weeks."

I wanted to take her home immediately, but they wanted to continue to monitor her throughout the day. The techs suggested I take care of any work-related things I had to do and come back at six o'clock to pick Kaspi up. I think there was some hidden meaning in that advice. "Wait before you take her home so we can see if she at least makes it through the day."

Those hours between drop-off and pickup were an absolute blur. I went home, took a shower, and went into work to tell them the facts. I would not be coming into the office—at all—for the next week and a half. I was already permitted to work from home most of the time, but it was a big ask for me to close my office doors for that long. I was in compliance and human resources, after all. Fortunately, it wasn't really an ask; it was a tell. About this same time, my boss (and the owner of the company) was struggling with his own personal and professional issues and didn't really have a clue what was happening in his company, so I wasn't reprimanded.

The week-and-a-half timeframe I set wasn't random. Throughout the day, I kept hearing it over and over again . . .

"Ten days . . . ten days."

I didn't exactly know the meaning behind the words, or what would happen once the countdown reached zero, but

I knew that would be the number of days I needed with Kaspi.

I filled the rest of my day running errands, both to help distract me and to ensure that I had absolutely no reason to leave the house for the next ten days. It was like stocking up on food in preparation for a major blizzard—or hurricane nowadays.

I returned to the vet around 5:30 PM—a little earlier than we had agreed upon, but what can I say? I was eager.

Kaspi had done well in my absence. No more seizures! This by no means meant she was in good condition.

"She's going to need a lot of care and attention," the vet told me. "Her hind legs aren't working for her right now, so she's going to need help with everything, including going outside."

Raul and I were going to have to help her get in and outside to go potty. They advised us to put a towel under her belly and pull up on it like a sling to help alleviate some of her weight as she tried to move around.

Thanks to the hours I had to kill before picking her up, there was a great Kaspi-friendly environment waiting for us back at the house. I set up camp in the living room, including an air mattress right next to an orthopedic dog bed so I could sleep right next to her. Every night, we would be situated right next to the sliding glass doors that lead into the backyard in case she needed to go outside. Since I knew she was going to have trouble walking, I even put out a throw rug on the tile floor to keep her from sliding around.

The moment we got home, with my help, Kaspi ambled over to her dog bed, laid down, and rested her head on the air mattress. That night, I told Raul, "Someone is going to be at this house every single minute of every day for the next ten days. We are not leaving her alone."

He didn't fight me on that.

Kinley was just as concerned as the rest of us. She would routinely walk up to Kaspi, smell her, circle her, and lay down next to her. Then, she would either lick (kiss) her or simply rest her head on top of her. Sometimes, although she stayed close enough to lay back-to-back with Kaspi, she would turn away. She was physically very close but mentally distant. It was like she wasn't sure if Kaspi was going to make it and wanted to be close while emotionally withdrawing.

I would always gauge if Kaspi was going to die or not based on which way Kinley's head was turned. It was like her level of engagement was a barometer. As time went on, we started to call her "Little Nurse Kinley." She earned this little nickname at night. Once an hour, like clockwork, Kinley would wake up out of a dead sleep, jump off of the bed, walk to the living room, circle Kaspi, lick her, smell her, then go back to bed. Those little check-ins became a highly regimented part of her routine.

For the next week and a half, I laid on the floor with Kaspi and played with energy. At night, sometimes Raul would take a shift on the floor while I slept in the bed, but it was mostly me spending time on the air mattress. I moved the energy and held space for her to heal, and I did it happily.

I seriously did not leave the house for ten days. There was no other place I wanted to be.

During those days, I focused on recalling some of the magic from my childhood—like the energy I could see and feel around people and animals. When Kaspi had come home, I saw areas of heavier energy around her. Part of the work I did involved moving my hands like paddles to pull that heavy energy away and replace it with golden energy from above. I knew this to be universal energy, God energy, source energy.

I understood that visualizing any process can help the

intended result be realized. So as strange as it sounds, I found one image and locked onto it as a way to picture what I was doing and bring it into the 3D. I imagined what looked like a giant tube of toothpaste squeezing out golden, sparkly light into Kaspi's energy field. I imagined that energy would go straight into her body and then surround her and fill up any dark, dense or congested energy that wasn't serving her. Once the spaces were filled, Kaspi's energetic field grew bigger and bigger.

Progress was slow and the Little Nurse Kinley barometer continued to waver for days. I constantly called on my grandma, angels, God, whoever I could think of for help. I bargained with them.

"If you just let Kasper pop up and live, I promise I'll never practice law again."

"I'll go to hot yoga every single day of my life, forever."

"If you let Kasper live, I'll never eat cake again."

. . . some promises are more reasonable than others.

Throughout this entire journey, I kept hearing the same thing.

"Ten days."

Kaspi was still drinking water and even occasionally going outside with my help. She wasn't eating, though.

On the eighth night, Raul was away for work and I was sleeping on the air mattress with Kinley by my side. Out of nowhere, an energy came into the room and woke me up. It was a beautiful, emerald, sparkly green energy. (I should clarify that I saw this in my mind's eye, not in the flesh.) I watched the energy move over to Kaspi and start to move around her tail and back legs. When it did, Kaspi's legs twitched. The light moved up to a position over her abdomen and she started breathing irregularly. It moved to her neck and head, and . . . you can guess what happened. Subtle, twitch-like responses.

All of a sudden, I started hearing a new message, over and over again. Instead of "ten days," this one was just a name.

"Raphael, Raphael, Raphael."

I had no idea what it meant. Soon, the green glow faded away, along with my consciousness as I slowly returned to sleep.

When I awoke the next morning, I did some research and all of the details fell into place. I wasn't very well-read on angels so I couldn't have known this without looking it up. Archangel Raphael is the angel of healing, and he's associated with Malachite—an emerald green, sparkly stone.

I guess that means he's one of my guys now . . .

I continued to call upon him for the rest of the day and into the night.

Before falling asleep, I thought to myself about how often I had heard "ten days." Here we were, pushing toward the end of day nine and Kaspi didn't seem to have made much progress. I made a promise to myself. If the tenth day rolled around and Kaspi still seemed to be sick and potentially suffering, I would make the difficult call and put her to sleep.

Day 10.

I woke up to see that she had gotten up and walked over to her water bowl to get a drink without any help or encouragement from me.

Okay. This is a good sign.

I was amazed as I watched her wander over to her food bowl and just stand there in front of it, expectantly. It had been so long since she had eaten anything other than the occasional treat that for a moment I didn't even consider that she was asking for food. When I poured out the kibble she immediately started chomping away. She finished the first bowl, so I gave her a second serving. Two bowls down, onto the third . . .

More, more, more.

It was like she was making up for all the meals she lost.

The human part of me was maintaining a sense of cautious optimism, struggling to believe Kaspi had made such a sudden turn around. My soul, though, expected nothing less.

I opened the back door and watched as she walked out into the backyard completely unassisted for the first time in a week and a half. I suppose on some level I downplayed these events not wanting to get my hopes up too high.

It's just like they say . . . before people or animals die, they give one final rally. That's what this is.

Maybe she would be gone by nightfall and my various bargains would fall through. Perhaps I wouldn't be giving up cake and law after all . . .

Let me explain something about Kaspi. She had originally been rescued by an elderly couple and trained as a therapy dog. Because of that training, she was incredibly calm. There was a lot of medical equipment in the home with her previous owners, and she had been trained never to go into a room without being put on a leash and lead through the doorway, for fear of damaging something vital.

After Raul and I brought Kaspi home for the first time, we immediately started teaching her to be naughty. We bribed her with treats to get her to jump onto the couch and the bed with us. Even though we were a laid-back and lawless household, we could never quite get Kaspi to master one thing: playing. She was a lazy dog—happy to eat, sleep, and be petted whenever possible.

At 3 PM on the tenth day of her recovery, she wandered

over to the back door, picked up one of her stuffed toys, and started tossing it up and throwing her front paws at it. She wasn't just recovered, she wasn't just rallying; Kaspi was back and better than ever. Kinley confirmed this by breaking into her "booty dance"—tossing her hips from one side to the other while pouncing with all her might.

"Alright. We're good!" I said, turning to Raul with an uncontrollable smile. "I think she's good!"

I'm sure we've all seen one rendition or another of that happy scene in *A Christmas Carol* where Ebenezer Scrooge wakes up on Christmas morning as a changed man with a second shot at life. That day with Kaspi's recovery was something like that for me.

That was it. I was done with law. I was now impervious to excuses. The time for "sticking it out" in corporate for reasons like money or what Raul might want me to do were over. I was done working for corporate, and I was done making myself and my dogs sick. It was currently April, and I knew that when I left Houston in December for my family Christmas in Pennsylvania, that would be the last paycheck I ever received from "The Man." In fact, it was going to be the last time I took any money for anything other than doing what I loved. But how was I going to pull that one off?

CHAPTER 8
Exit Strategy

❧

I N THE PAST, I had gone through health coaching programs and even been certified, but never with the intention of actually starting my own business. Anything I had ever done in healing was done because I wanted to work on myself. Some part of me was convinced for years that this was never something I would be able to do for a living. Now, I was ready to press the mute button on that voice and move forward into the great unknown of healing work.

"That's it. I'm done," I told Raul after Kaspi's recovery. "I'm going to become an animal intuitive and coach."

Raul looked intrigued. "A coach?" He asked. "What kind of coach?"

"A mentor. I'm going to help people reach a higher version of themselves. You know, break out of their boxes and find a better life."

He nodded at the description. "Alright. Whatever you wanna do, I've got your back. I'm going to support you."

I was surprised at how easy the conversation had been, feeling like I was getting away with murder. "Cool," I said, and started to walk away.

"Just make sure you replace your corporate salary within a year."

I stopped. "Dude, seriously?" I started throwing all the resistance I could muster at him. "Building a business takes time. Most businesses *lose* money the first couple of years, don't they?"

He nodded. "Most businesses, yeah, but didn't you just say you're going to help people break out of their boxes?"

I got ready to come back swinging hard with a counter-argument, but realized I didn't have one. All I did was slump a little and say, "Oh, shit."

The defense rests, your honor.

My excuses were just more naysaying on my part. In fact, it was this type of belief system that got me exactly where I was—sick, tired, and full of regret.

There had to be another way.

This was the mindset I held as I began my transition away from corporate and into the person I am today. What would be required for me to leave my job and keep (or go beyond) my corporate salary?

How do I do that?

Like so many endeavors, I had to start out with expanding my mind. That meant lots and lots of books. I remember I was reading Elizabeth Gilbert's *Big Magic* when something clicked; I was inspired and pleasantly surprised to learn how much her unique perspective about creativity resonated with my own journey.

From there, I decided to use my intuition to seek out teachings and teachers. Sometimes I would simply go to Barnes and Noble and meander through the different sections until whatever I needed to read popped out at me. I called it "scanning." Any book that caught my attention, I would pick up, touch, feel, and explore the vibe I received.

Other times I'd surf the net until I landed on something that resonated. On my laptop, I'd simply run my hand over the picture and feel the energy radiating from the screen. Be it mindset or spirituality or quantum physics, the lessons I needed were usually right there in front of me.

All it took to make this process effective was for me to be receptive and open to my own feelings.

Being open and receptive helped me find and understand the tools I needed to make this bold transition. *Using* those tools took a different kind of effort. If I was going to succeed, it would take more than simple New Age thinking. Sure, the spiritual and religious movement hit the nail on the head with some coined terms like "peace and love," but I always thought it was missing key pieces from actual teachings, and those were the gaps that I sought to fill.

This wasn't going to be a matter of "thinking happy thoughts" and watching them materialize before my very eyes. In fact, I didn't relate to any of the New Age teachings I stumbled across; I knew my journey would have to take me much further into the past, straight to ancient spiritual texts and early 1900s teachings on prosperity.

This realization came at a time when "prosperity" seemed like it couldn't be further from reach. Things at work had taken a turn for the worst. It was beginning to seem that my old life was going to go down kicking and screaming. As I mentioned before, the CEO of my company had been struggling with addiction and was a corrupt and scheming individual. Still, despite his issues, he was capable of putting on a friendly face and behaving like a kind, old man that at times, was reasonable and relatively pleasant to be around. Unfortunately, before I could leave the job, he went on sabbatical. In his place he left, well, let's just call this man "Bane"—after the bane of my existence.

Bane had no qualifications for the job of managing the

office beyond the fact that he was the CEO's friend. Whereas my former boss would keep the worst of himself away from me, Bane laid it all out on the table. He was openly sexist and thought he knew everything despite the fact that he had no formal schooling, experience, or training that qualified him to run a company. He wore a gun on his hip, chewed tobacco, and made a regular habit of spitting it out into a Styrofoam cup right in front of me.

Bane was the embodiment of everything I despised about Texas. Yes, my feelings were immature and negative but at the time I thought I had good reason to hate the place. You see, Texas (the land itself) hated me back, and I'm not just saying this! The news came to me through a referral from a friend.

"You have to go see Regina," she said. "She's an intuitive healer, you just go and sit on her couch and she tells you everything that's wrong with you and how to fix it."

I made an appointment right away.

Before meeting with Regina, she knew nothing about me but my name. However, right away, she explained that she could feel how the land in Texas was repelling me.

"Yeah. No shit Texas is repelling me," I said. "And I fucking hate it, too. Everyone in it, everything about it."

. . . I guess you could say I had some pent-up feelings on the matter.

Regina took my outburst with surprising grace. She nodded and said, "I get it. I can see that." Then she asked, "Do you wanna let that go?"

"No! I don't need to let that go! I need to get the hell out of here!"

"I can help with that, too."

That gave my racing rage a flat tire. I calmed myself before asking, "Okay . . . what can you tell me?"

She simply said, "You're the White man, now."

What the hell?

Seeing the confusion on my face, she delved into the deeper explanation.

"In almost all of your past lives, you've been a female and a Native American. You—" stopping suddenly, she turned to empty space and said to seemingly no one, "No, I'm not going to ask her that."

She was doing something I would later learn was called "channeling," which meant calling upon her spiritual advisors and communicating with them.

"Ask me what?" I asked.

She shrugged. "They want me to ask you why one of your legs is shorter than the other."

That one caught me off guard. Like I said, she knew nothing about me but my name, and yet somehow she had already called out this thing that hardly anyone else knew about. My right leg is over one inch longer than the left. She wrapped the reason for this into her explanation of her "White man" comment. In one of my prior lives, I'd been a White male fighting for the Confederacy; the only lifetime where I was a man, she said. She went on to say that during the war, my left knee cap was shot off which manifests today as a shorter leg.

Now, my problem with Texas was two-fold. On the one hand, the land was rejecting me because of my race. It was paying me back for the role I played in the Civil War. The flip side of this issue was something I viewed as a little bit too crazy.

"How long have you been co-mingling with Native American DNA? Have you slept with or had a relationship with anyone of Hispanic descent?"

That piqued my interest. My last three romantic

relationships had been with men that fit that description—Cuban, Honduran, and Mexican. I told her this and she nodded. Her explanation of my Texas problem was mind-opening.

"Your relationships with those men have reactivated the Native American DNA from your ancestry. Now, the land is rejecting you because you've come back as the 'White man.'"

In a strange way, it made sense. Though I'm White and have always been around White people, when I began working in corporate in Texas, it was almost as though my opinion of the "White man" changed overnight. I felt as though every White business man or woman around me was a greedy racist. Still, could something like this be explained with what Regina just told me? How could she possibly know this?

She proved her ability to inexplicably know things with the next thing she said.

"Oh, by the way. Do you want to fix the issues you're having with your thyroid and magnesium levels?"

The fact that she had any idea at all that I was even having these issues was amazing. But her suggested treatment seemed almost other-worldly to me. I had been trying all kinds of medical approaches and seeing little to no effects.

"Okay, stop all of that," she said. "It won't work because you're not like most humans. What we're going to do is download everything you need directly into your body."

After a little bit of resistance from me over the basic physics that should prevent anything like that from working, I gave it a try. Lo and behold, where all of the other medical treatments had failed, her method succeeded. This was all part of the first kind of many intuitive techniques that I would study, and it was called ThetaHealing®.

There was much to learn and little time to learn it.

My corporate d-date of December 16, 2016, was rapidly approaching and I was still unsure of my next move. Fortunately, it wasn't necessary for me to see too far into the future. I had my intuition, and as long as I listened and kept following it, I knew I couldn't be steered wrong. I resolved that if there was a training or retreat opportunity my gut told me to attend, I would commit to it and worry about the home and work consequences later. I have to admit, Bane's continued rampage through my office made it *very* easy for me to disregard my work and follow my intuition.

My meeting with Regina had sparked a major interest in ThetaHealing®, and it also made me want to get in touch with my ancestry. I started searching for a retreat that could guide me in those directions. Of course, Raul had trouble distinguishing retreats from vacations, and at one point joked that I should go on a retreat to learn to cook if I was going to be working from home (my idea of cooking is homemade nut milk and homemade granola or anything that can be whipped up in a Vitamix®).

Finding the right opportunity seemed like a tall order, which meant I had to start digging right away. Much like my scanning, my search involved a lot of time sitting in front of a computer until something inside me said, "Yes."

At one point, I walked away from the screen for a break. When I came back, it was somehow open to a page about a retreat at a resort in New Mexico. It involved hikes, sweat lodges, and all the things that I felt I needed to feed my soul. Part of the retreat even involved working with two internationally known Native American chiefs. If that's not divine guidance, I'm not sure what is.

The idea of strenuous hiking concerned me just a little. I was struggling with the weight I had gained during the lost years, and I wanted to be sure I could handle what this retreat was going to throw at me. So, I called the resort and asked about hikes in the area. The woman on the other end of the line put me at ease; they didn't have anything more intense on the resort grounds than a few short hills. Okay, I could do that, no problem.

Well, it was only once I arrived at the retreat that I discovered the hikes didn't take place on the resort grounds. Some days, we hopped onto a bus, rode to a big boulder, and hiked along a rocky trail to get to the top for a view of petroglyphs that had been left there long ago. It was one of the greater challenges I faced on the trip, and therefore one of the most rewarding experiences. At the end of each hike, I felt stronger and more confident about whatever lay ahead of me. I wasn't going to be the first person to the top, but I also made sure that I wouldn't be the last.

As I expected, the most illuminating part of the trip took place in the sweat lodge. In complete darkness, we sat and began to sing songs. Songs I had never heard before but somehow knew all of the words. Then there were moments when my body seemed to move automatically, performing movements that my mind never learned but my body somehow already knew. It was all so familiar, it was a sense of total remembrance.

There were multiple ceremonies or rounds to the sweat lodge. Between each one, we'd open the tent flaps and the Chief would reach in with a long shovel and add hot stones (which represented the Great Spirit or Grandfathers) to the pit in the center of the lodge. My vision was blurry, partly because of the sweat and tears in my eyes and partly because I was not wearing my glasses or contacts. For most of the experience, I was as blind as a bat; however, on one occasion when the flaps opened and the Chief lowered the scorching stones, I saw an incredible image with crystal clarity.

The thing I am about to describe was much more than an intuitive download. Typically, I see or hear things in the sense of a sudden knowing, a vision within my third eye, or at most as projected images in my peripheral vision. As the Chief opened up the tent flap, I saw behind him what can only be described as a glimpse into an alternate dimension. Beyond the tent lay an enchanted fairy forest. I knew that this was not a mere dream or vision; I was looking through a genuine opening into another dimension. It was so real that, if I chose to, I would have been able to walk out of that tent and into that magical place.

Of course, that was one walk I wouldn't be taking. I've always preferred to keep my body planted firmly in this world. Besides, the beautiful reality I was witnessing already had its own Keveney, in a sense.

There were two elementals in that forest—a fairy and a gnome. Intuitively, I knew who these two characters really were. Within this alternate reality, I was the fairy. My old boyfriend, C, was the gnome. Seeing our two beings intertwined in their playful games helped me to understand that he and I had some kind of soul contract, something that would keep his energy coming and going from my life for a long time.

I would go on to have many teachers in my life, and that glimpse into another realm helped me understand that C was one of them. He had introduced me to a free-spirited lifestyle upon my arrival in Texas, years ago. If not for those lessons of embodying child-like wonder, having no agenda, and floating down the river of life, I might not have seen my work in corporate for what it was—miserable. I would have had nothing to compare it to.

By the time I left the retreat in New Mexico, I had gained exactly what I went there seeking. It wasn't just a clearer understanding of how I was going to make my transition out of corporate, but *why* it must happen. There was so much more to life than what I was currently doing, and it was time to look beyond the four walls of the tiny box I had put myself in.

This was a phase of dramatic ebbs and flows, and returning to the office after that wonderful trip was just as draining as you might think. Bane was intensely micro-managing an office that he barely understood. His corruption became readily apparent when I realized that instead of firing people he didn't agree with, he simply harassed them into quitting their jobs so that he wouldn't have to pay them unemployment. For the people who stuck it out and left Bane with no choice but to fire them, he had the gall to tell me to falsify reports so that it appeared the employees had been terminated due to their own incompetence. This, along with many other things, I refused to do.

Standing up to Bane didn't exactly make me a shining star in his eyes.

Thus was the beginning of a paper trail I built to protect myself. Bane would send an email instructing me to do something unethical; I would respond with a firm "no" and state my reasons, then I stashed the correspondence away for later use.

Through all the months of struggling against the finale of my corporate lifestyle, I had one great light at the end of the tunnel. Everything was in place for me to take a three-week course in ThetaHealing® in Fort Worth, Texas.

Months earlier, when the previous CEO of our company had given me permission to work with a remote, modified schedule for these three weeks, I paid for the course and reserved my Airbnb. Even still, despite the fact that I had this agreement in writing, Bane wasn't having it. He told me I would no longer be permitted to work from home at all, let alone for almost a month. At first, it was difficult for me to understand what his problem was. The work would still be getting done; nothing would change.

It didn't take me long to put two and two together. In addition to being a bad manager, Bane simply didn't like me because I stood up to him. He was taking out his personal feelings on me in any way he could.

Still, I had no idea what I was supposed to do about my upcoming course. Being AWOL from a job for over three weeks was certainly grounds to be fired, and fired just the way that Bane would want it done—with cause. Sure, I would be leaving the job on my own terms within a few months, but I had plans for those final paychecks.

I reminded myself of my own resolution.

Follow your intuition; do you, and don't worry about anything else.

That settled it. I was going to the training.

The seminar not only provided training in an area of healing I was interested, it also helped dredge up my struggles and kickstart the journey of sorting through them. The educational aspect was fascinating. We went through different organs and systems within the human body and learned about the energies associated with them. The reproductive system, digestive system, cardiovascular system . . . all of these are tied to their own specific kind of energy. When the energy becomes congested, so does the physical body.

I had some minor doubts in my teacher's legitimacy because of her tendency to judge others by their astrology charts instead of intuitive messages, but those doubts were removed the day that she called me out for my unresolved stuff with a man in my life. As she described the physical characteristics of this man, I hoped she was referring to my husband (but my gut knew otherwise). When she said, "green eyes," my heart sunk, and I knew she was describing C perfectly. She described our energies as intertwined and recommended I reach out to him for closure. In fact, she told me not to return to class until I did. I immediately felt resistance and came up with excuses why I couldn't (and shouldn't) complete this task. She wasn't taking no for an answer; she even found his phone number online after I told her I no longer had it.

After nearly ten years of radio silence, C and I spoke on the phone that night. We quickly fell into natural conversation. For a moment, it was like no time had passed.

I told him about the seminar, what I was going through, and why I called him. He listened all the way through and at one point said, "If your figuring all that out has anything to do with me, I'm still waiting."

I was surprised at his response and didn't really know what to make of it. I remember panicking a little inside. I quickly changed the subject, and we talked for a little while longer, updating each other on our lives.

At one point C told me he was "retired," I couldn't help but feel confused, and it showed in my reply.

"But, you're a year younger than me, and I'm only 34."

"Well, I made different life choices than you," C said. "I didn't run off and get married."

Touché.

At first I thought he was trying to pick a fight, but that wasn't the kind of guy C was. I was caught off guard by his comment and not sure how to take it. Luckily, he followed up with a kind-hearted outpouring. "When things ended, I never meant you any harm. I only want the best for you." There was silence on the other end of the line for a moment before he continued. "We're both older and hopefully wiser now, and I'd like to think that I'd have handled things differently knowing what I know now." He also clarified that his "retirement" was more of a sabbatical.

I didn't know what to say. It was a nice note to go out on, and the conversation soon drifted to a close.

I wouldn't call it closure, but I gathered that the lesson here was for me to live in the moment. It certainly seemed to have worked out okay for C. Maybe I should give it a try.

We humans spend so much time in regret over the past and worry about the future, and we miss living life to its fullest.

ThetaHealing® only scratched the surface of what I would go on to learn. As nice as it would have been to build the knowledge required for a successful business in a quick few weeks, my studying and learning would have to continue. They continue to this day. I went on to study Reiki, Quantum-Touch, and so much more. It was my voracious appetite for knowledge and healing that kept me moving.

Once I got back to the office, things were largely unchanged. Bane was still micromanaging and puffing his chest, and I still had my job; I guess he needed me too bad to let me go. He had thrown his temper tantrum, but it was all bark and no bite. We continued to clash heads.

In one of our final brawls, he walked up to my desk and threw down a packet of paperwork and accused me of making mistakes by failing to list all of the states in which we were licensed to work.

"Yeah," I said. "I didn't list the licenses that we don't have."

"I don't care. We will have them, eventually."

"And when that day comes," I said, "I'll make sure the paperwork reflects that."

"Don't be such a lawyer," he *actually* said. "Just fill it out the right way."

"Get us licensed, and I *will* fill it out the right way."

This back-and-forth continued right up until it escalated

by Bane slamming his hands down on my desk and issuing the command. "You are going to do this!"

I shot out of my seat and stood on my toes so that I could meet him eye-to-eye, then slammed my fists on my desk, only louder.

"No. I'm. NOT!"

Our risk manager came into my office a moment later.

"I could hear you two screaming through the walls," she said. "Drop what you're doing. You're going to the hospital right now."

"Why?" I asked, still fuming.

"Because your face is tomato-red and I can see your heart beating through your chest. I'm worried you're going to have a stroke."

I resisted her for a while before agreeing that it would probably be best if I had some professionals take a look at me. When I got to the hospital, they told me that my blood pressure was through the roof and forbade me from going back to work that day—or the rest of the week. That was one treatment plan that I happily accepted.

There were only three weeks left until I planned to exit corporate once and for all. I had originally planned to give notice the following week. However, that day at the hospital changed my mind. I decided I wouldn't be giving the professional courtesy of any notice. I stayed home for a couple days and then returned to the office for my final weeks of work.

On December 16, 2016, I sent an e-mail to Bane and the CEO that clearly laid out my reasons for leaving without notice. By this point, I had stockpiled such an incredible paper trail of them requesting me to commit fraudulent acts that I dared him to try and mess with me. I had no intention of filing for unemployment before that day at the hospital. I didn't need or want the money, but I did want to make them pay for what they did to me and countless others before me. I knew I had a strong case for constructive termination, and the lawyer (and need to be right) in me wanted justice. As I predicted, they fought my claim for unemployment, and as I predicted, I won. Perhaps this final conflict was a negative way to leave but we all have our human moments, and this one felt particularly good. I'd had my way with those good ole boys once and for all.

CHAPTER 9
From the Inside, Out

T HAT WAS IT! Freedom!
I was free of the corporate lifestyle, free of the stress,
free of the high blood pressure and thoughts of rage.
Unfortunately, I was also without my corporate paycheck
and paying clients. Pressure from Raul to replace my income
was continuing to mount. The expression, "You're not out of
the woods yet," has some application here. I could feel the
sun on my face and hear the wind blowing in the grass. That
didn't change the fact that there was still a massive (albeit
beautiful) mountain that stood before me.

Now that I had freshly landed in the world beyond
corporate, I was in a phase of my life where my ascent to
the life I always wanted required me to both expand my
consciousness and improve my circumstances. I knew that
much of this could be done in solitude, but I also knew that a
great deal of growth can come from working with a mentor.

So, I hired a business coach. You have to spend money
to make money, right? As things would turn out, hiring
her as a coach was really the result of lingering corporate
thought processes. Although I liked her personally, she was
what I would call a very 3D, traditional business coach,

interested in methodically building a business step-by-step. Professionally, she was a woman of systems, hours, phone calls, desk time, and the "pay-to-play" model. What does that remind you of?

Still stuck in my attachment to corporate thinking, I thought I needed an office address to be viewed as legitimate. I went and rented a shared workspace to improve my professional image. This, of course, was just a story I was telling myself. Ultimately, having an office turned out to be crucial, just not that office and not for those reasons. Because my motivation was off-kilter, the space didn't pay off. By its very nature, a shared space means that anyone can end up using the room the day before you. Since I couldn't control the energy in the room, I had to spend a lot of time just to clear the office before I could work with clients. I still hung onto the shared space, though, because my mindset and business coach were both still pushing me in the direction of corporate thinking.

It all seemed so unnecessary. Why did I have to go through so many steps which felt like chores as well as all these added expenses? Why couldn't I just come up with my own high-level program, quickly sign someone, and continue on with a 90% close rate on future clients? Those were my desirable numbers, so what was I doing toiling away with all of these steps?

My initial goal was to make enough so that I could handle my law school loan payments each month; that would at least be enough to keep Raul at bay while I figured out the way forward. That meant clearing in excess of $2,000 a month.

I had to start small. Before I reached the point where I was well-enough-known to be receiving calls out of the blue regarding pets and animals, I built a base of clients in a different, more personal way. This was how I found my first client.

Anna was already a good friend of mine, and as with so many of my friends, I received an intuitive hit every time I saw her or thought of her. As my confidence in my abilities grew, I described to her the vision I had whenever I was with her, even though it was rather awkward.

Three pink roses and congestion around her pelvis. When I say congestion, I mean that I saw dense energy and flashing lights where her ovaries would be—like they were lighting up to send her a message.

When I described this image to her, she started to cry.

Unbeknownst to me, she had been pregnant with triplets a long time ago. Midway through her pregnancy, she experienced a life-threatening health crisis. She lived, but her babies did not survive.

This experience rocked her to her core. Despite working with a grief counselor shortly following the event, she felt like she never truly processed the grief or healed. She shared with me there was one thing she had agreed to do in counseling, plant a rose bush for each baby. However for whatever reason—most likely avoiding the pain—by the time I told her about my intuitive image, she had yet to plant the flowers. I suggested that she go purchase three flowers and plant them at her home. She agreed and planted the rose bushes in less than two weeks. Later, I paid her a visit to see the flowers and commemorate the triplets and her healing.

Anna soon became my first client to enroll in a multiple month coaching package.

I remember at the start of one session she mentioned some challenges at home. Her immediate experience of her husband was that he was always worried about some physical ailment or impending health crisis; she described this as him seeing the glass half-empty while she saw it half-full. She felt like the energy in the house was becoming heavy, and it was difficult to get her husband to see the positive side of things.

We talked a bit about universal law. I told her, "We can only receive that which we can expect." So, if she expected her husband to come home, be miserable, and complain about his aches and pains, that's exactly what she was going to get.

I asked her, "What do you want to do today?"

She didn't know at first but eventually realized how much she wanted to go into the city and get some fresh veggies and seafood.

"Spend the morning," I told her. "Go to the market, gather ingredients for a meal. Be grateful, smell the smells, handle the fruits. See the beauty around you. When you get home and cook for your husband, focus on the idea of him coming home and having a positive reaction." I asked her to picture him talking about how amazing the food was, that he'd been craving exactly what she cooked, that the veggies she prepared were the freshest he'd tasted in a while, and that he'd thank her.

"Yeah," Anna said with a subtle roll of her eyes. "That's not going to happen."

"Not if you don't expect it to," I replied.

We weren't practicing mind control, and she didn't have a magic ability to make her husband come home as a different person. The truth is, we all have high and low vibe energy inside of us. These different energies can play off of each other. If my client sat at home thinking negatively and feeding these low vibrations and her husband was at work all day with similar frequencies of doubt, fear, or pain running in his energy, those thoughts would be triggered as soon as he walked in the door. Especially with married couples, a seed of doubt can very quickly grow into a perfect doubt storm.

Anna called me that night . . .

"You will not believe it! He walked in, and . . ." she repeated the words that I had told her to imagine him saying . . . "He even asked if I wanted to go for a walk, and . . ." her happiness kept rolling, as did her new mode of thinking. (It would be irresponsible for me to move on without noting that Anna had been doing a lot of internal work for several months which certainly contributed to the happy outcome in this scenario; it was more than positive thoughts and wishful thinking that resulted in the harmony she experienced with her hubby that night.)

I was thrilled, so happy to see our work pay off in such a rewarding way. Unfortunately, one client wasn't going to pay my bills, and it certainly wasn't going to help me meet Raul's request that I replace my corporate salary within a year.

After a few months of working with my very corporate-like business coach, things still weren't going the way I wanted, and I adopted another faulty mindset: I didn't need to do anything different, I just needed to do or buy more of what I was already doing. My coach invited me and some of her other clients to attend a conference in Florida put on by another coaching company. These folks initially seemed like a good fit—and for another hefty investment, I could hire them on top of my current coach.

More, more, more.

Foolproof, right?

I completed the questionnaires and had my credit card out—ready to sign yet another contract. As I put pen to paper, my current coach and potential new one got into an argument. They were fighting over me, *right in front of me!* One was airing out the dirty laundry of the other. It seemed so unethical, or what I call "out of integrity." I completely lost interest in both parties.

I received an intuitive download that said, "Take the

contract and credit card off the table. Get outside. Take a walk. Hug a tree. Get grounded. Go."

It was sound advice, and I followed it happily. After a little bit of a stroll, some breathing, and relaxing, I found a table that was covered in beautiful crystal bracelets. The woman behind the table radiated a healing and loving energy. She suddenly asked, "You know animals are your conduit for healing people, right?"

Finally . . . After all of my work with animals and belief in my ability to heal, after all the people that told me the two didn't go together . . . finally here was this gorgeous stranger telling me exactly what I knew and longed for confirmation about. It goes without saying that she didn't remain a stranger for very long (in fact, she quickly because a great friend and soul sister who wrote the Foreword to this very book). She sent me in the right direction and gave me the phone number of her friend and mentor who she was sure could help me with my situation, we'll call her Dharma.

Dharma was also a business coach, but in the intuitive and spiritual way that I knew would best serve me. I instantly wanted to hire her, but there was some internal resistance. I was still riled up by the two coaches that started arguing right in front of me, and for a while, all I did was spout reasons why I shouldn't spend more money on myself or my business. Of course, I had my own need to be right and faulty beliefs playing in my head, including fear and judgment around the $50,000 price tag on Dharma's website.

"Well I already spent $12,000, and I'm clearly not getting *that* back." I stubbornly wanted to get back the value that I put into this person, if not in cash then through her own hard work. I couldn't fathom hiring yet another coach and spending more money. How could I be sure this time would work out for me and my business?

After about a month of following Dharma on social

media and listening to a few of her webinars, I sent her a text message. I explained where I got her number and how I resonated so much with the way she spoke about intuition, mindset, and expanding our consciousness. She immediately suggested we hop on a call, and we did. I knew instantly that I had to work with her privately—my soul said yes, but my human feared the large investment. I took a deep breath (and a leap of faith), and I said yes to her offer to begin private coaching. It was a knowing like when Kaspi had her seizure; intuitively I knew that there was no other choice but to jump now and figure out how to pay back my credit card later.

A few weeks into our relationship, Dharma asked, "How much longer are you going to let that story about the other coaches dictate your life and keep you from making money right now?"

I shrugged. She was right. I was giving my current circumstances power by playing right into them.

Dharma went on. "You have a choice to make. If you want, you can continue working with that coach also for another four or five months until your contract is up just because you want to challenge her and make her wrong. Or—" She stopped and considered her next question. "How much did you spend?"

I danced around the question, talking about all of my expenses on top of the $12k.

"Just give me a number."

"$15k," I blurted out. As far as estimations of how much money I had put into that current coach and her philosophy, that one was probably a little low.

"Great," Dharma said. "And how much are you hoping to make this month?"

"I don't know," I said. "Five thousand dollars would be great."

"Alright. Then here is what you're going to do. Put those numbers together. You're going to make $20,000 this month, mark this chapter of your life complete, forgive and be grateful, and never talk about this experience again. You simply have to move past this story."

Obviously, I was floored at even the idea of making that much money in one month. It sounded ridiculous. How could it even be possible? I never made that much in one month as a lawyer.

This was a major turning point for me. I had already heard a thousand times that consistent action yields consistent results. One of the early lessons I received from Dharma expanded on that principle: Consistent energy yields consistent action. That meant that if I held onto doubt or fear, feelings that I was not worthy, or the need to be right, then all I was going to do was hit resistance and stay in the spin without making any progress—or money.

I was shocked (with myself and the Universe itself) when the end of the next month rolled around and I ended up hitting the goal that Dharma had helped me set. I worked hard and took big action, and , I know that hitting the goal was a direct result of the internal work I'd done and letting go of my attachment to the old coach.

Although my goal had been met, the process wasn't sustainable. It was only a taste of what *could* be. I wanted to keep expanding, but *my stuff* kept coming up. This began the delicate dance I started to perform, working on myself, then working with clients at a higher level, then working on myself again.

. . . *Rinse, repeat.*

One such expansion of my consciousness came with recognizing what money truly is—an energy on the planet. It wasn't just something that could be spent on fancy bags and high-end cars. To me, money became part of the path to prosperity. I had to look at financial well-being as part of my own holistic health. There are many practitioners out there that want to heal the world and make it a better place while getting paid in twigs and berries—I have to admit there was a time this sounded good to me, too. I had to accept that it was okay to want more, and there was no reason to make money itself "wrong."

This led to another key insight: Quality over quantity.

Even as a young adult, when purses were a crucial status symbol, I always opted for one classic $400 Coach purse over a selection of ten or twelve cheaper options. It was natural that I would apply the same mindset for my business. Rather than have a ton of clients who pay very little, I want a specific clientele willing to do deeper work and invest more time, energy, and resources. Of course, I knew I'd have to deliver a higher level of service and bigger results, too.

I heard many coaches talk about designing a system that makes them money in their sleep. They often want to reach as wide a network of clients as possible and have little bits of money trickling in from all directions. Intuitively, I knew that I would be happier and of greater use to my clients if I did my best to stick to one-on-one sessions and small groups.

This belief was further enforced when I heard stories from clients who attended large-scale motivational or personal development seminars where the crowd is whisked into a euphoric state or encouraged to walk over fire to prove that they can conquer all fears and obstacles.. These clients shared how they would attend these grand events, feel absolutely incredible for about a week or maybe even a month, then hit the lowest low of their lives. Why? Because the results were not sustainable. It's easy to go somewhere and drop into a flow state when you're surrounded by hundreds or thousands of people chanting, walking on coals, dancing, and feeding off each other's energy. When people attend those types of events, it's easy to merge as one and feel good. Upon return to regular life, they often crash. They haven't solved and resolved their own limiting energies and beliefs or embodied the highest teachings at the soul level.

Sure, I'm open to reaching and helping as many humans as I'm able. If, however, I had to choose between having a positive, short-term effect on millions of people or helping hundreds of people take quantum leaps in money, health, relationships, and creativity and create sustainable transformation, I'd choose the latter. So, I decided to design my business with this idea in mind and work at an intimate and high level with every client.

In the beginning, some clients came to me by way of their animals. I'd receive a call to help a sick dog or cat (or horse, or bunny, or guinea pig, or cow . . . you get the picture), and while I worked on the animal, I'd receive many messages about the human. Many of these messages came in the form of pictures of unresolved trauma from childhood or broken relationships, beliefs that limited their prosperity or energetic causes for their pet and/or their physical ailments, etc.

"Holy crap, how do you know that?" This was the typical response I would receive. From there, they would ask me what else I knew, and more importantly, what I could help them solve. This led me to working with the humans as well as their animals. The most fascinating thing was that the animal's illness or disruptive behavior almost always disappeared after the owners took responsibility for their lives and opened to a new way of being, doing, and having.

There were, of course, a good many people who loved their animals but were not ready to take responsibility for their own stuff. Essentially, they just wanted the opportunity to talk to their pets and know what their pets needed to heal or to stop an undesirable behavior.

"That's great, but I don't want to know about me."

No problem. I was happy to tap into their pet's energy once a week or month or so and do some healing work and communication.

I was getting more clients and delivering more value, which I loved. But I wasn't exactly receiving more in my bank account. Not exactly what I originally intended with quality over quantity; I was delivering increased service and results to more people, but I was afraid to ask for more money.

It was about this time that Dharma began encouraging me to increase my prices and charge my value. I resisted because I hadn't yet healed my own relationship with money. I had twisted beliefs about poverty being virtuous and "super" wealthy people being greedy. Evidently, I'd created arbitrary distinctions about how much was too much.

"Ask your clients," Dharma said. "Ask them what they would have paid you for the results they received."

I decided to approach my first client, Anna, with this question. Since working out her struggle with her husband, we had worked on healing trauma from her past, creating a new dynamic with her husband, securing a new job for her husband on the East Coast, and a cross-country move which also included selling her house for more than the asking price.

"Just curious," I said to her one day. "How much would you have paid for the results you received?"

The answer that I got was more than illuminating.

"Anything," she said . . . "I would have paid anything for this."

Okay, then . . .

Dharma then asked me how much money I invested in myself to become a better coach and healer. It was another illuminating answer. I was paying Dharma handsomely; I'd invested tens of thousands of dollars on healing and energy training (not to mention that first business coach); I was using skills that I paid dearly for in college and law school; I was paying contractors to help me with my website, social media, and public relations; and I was still paying for that office I wasn't using. That begged the question: If I was investing that much money in myself and my business, why wouldn't other people?

All of that looped straight back to the negative beliefs I had regarding money. Somewhere along the line, often through misguided religious training, we humans take on a belief that being poor is a virtue; this couldn't be farther from spirituality or Truth. Personally, and I have no idea where I picked up this notion, I believed that becoming "super" wealthy would mean that I lost connection to the world. I also believed I had to choose between love and money. (Sidebar: I see now it was no coincidence that C and I broke up literally the evening after my first day working in corporate.)

Working with Dharma, I learned that money is NOT the root of all evil. Money just *is*. It exists. It is neither good nor bad. The "evil" part is the relationship some humans have with money—it's our attachment to it that creates energetic congestion and harm. To thrive, we must let go of attachment. I had to be happy and grateful both with money and without it.

After I revised my offerings and raised my rates, the cycle reset; I had to go internal and resolve my own limiting energy and beliefs again. If I was going to request more money, I had to be open to receiving more of it. I began to embrace that my external world was a perfect carbon copy of my internal energetics. If I was upset with anything in the outside world—annoyed with the way a client was acting, frustrated with Raul, or hurt by a friend—if there was *anything* that I wasn't happy with—it wasn't anyone else's fault. It meant that there was a seed of that within me. The only way to clear the external was to clear it within, first.

There were times this process of personal growth was a lonely one. Out of all the creatures in the animal kingdom, we humans require the most and lengthiest care after we exit the womb and enter the world. We all have the need to be right—it's what protects us and keeps us safe—and we cling very tightly to things that give us love. They become our beliefs, and our beliefs become our truth.

For example, one habit I had to break was using other people as an excuse to *not* do something. Whenever I asked Raul if he wanted to go on a vacation, he would launch into one of his more common forms of resistance—lack. "How much does it cost? Should we spend that kind of money? Can your business pay for it?"

I'd answer his questions, fight with him because we actually had more than enough money to take whatever vacation we wanted, and make him wrong. I'd then blame him for me not going on the trips I wanted to take instead of simply saying, "Okay, cool. He's not interested. This is something I want to do; I can do it. What's stopping me?"

I created more time for myself to study ancient spiritual texts, Vedanta philosophy, and old prosperity teachings; meditate; clear my energy; and do deep, internal work. I was required to observe and remain curious about where I experienced congestion in my prosperity (which I define to include health, wealth, love, and spirituality) and remember not to judge or point fingers at anyone, including myself— even though I know I'm responsible for whatever I'd created (or not created). This was tricky at times.

To cope with the loneliness that sometimes surfaced when I did this work, I reverted back to things that didn't require a lot of human contact. I spent a great deal of time with the dogs, doing yoga, and going places I wanted to go regardless if Raul or my friends came along.

With that mindset, I was able to continue my leap-frogging pattern of improvement.

Expand self.

Expand business.

Repeat.

It was during this time in my life that my childhood experience with time travel and my trip to the mysterious Oasis Bar and Grill reached out to me again. Over the years, people in my life had different takes on what it actually meant. My dad was the only one to placidly view the event as an alien abduction and move on without issue. My girlfriends, the ones who were with me that night, would occasionally retell the story from their perspective.

"Dude, you were *GONE.*"

They always pushed me to do some research and see if there had been any place called the Oasis Bar and Grill in that area. I still hadn't, maybe because I was afraid of what I might find. Of course, it didn't matter if I was searching or not. That night would find me again and again.

I was at another convention in Florida when I was approached by a woman. She told me that she was a Reiki Master from Connecticut, and quickly said, "I've had a near-death experience, just like you. Tell me about yours."

Well, that's weird. Last time I checked I haven't had one of those.

I started to tell her that I never had a near-death experience, but she didn't even let me finish.

"Oh, yes you have. I've had multiple, and even floated above my body once when I was a child. Now, whenever I meet people who have had one of their own, I can tell."

I immediately thought that this woman was crazier than me, until the next thing she said.

"Your heart stopped. Something strange happened, but you remember it as a time travel story."

I was filled with excitement! Finally, someone could yield some answers on what happened to me back in the ninth grade. Unfortunately, she didn't have much to say, other than confirming that it happened. She took the conversation in a very interesting direction.

"There's a dark energy taking over this event," she said. "It's attached to one of the speakers."

I had to raise an eyebrow at that one. Personally, I'm not into playing around with dark energies. I believe they exist, but I choose not to open myself to them. I told her that, but she didn't stop. She said that I had the power to help, or rather, someone she called my spirit guide did.

"She dresses in purple and black, her name is Esmeralda. We need to call on her to clear the energy of this space. She's very powerful and can help us remove anything that is not from the light. You've met her before."

I thought of the robust woman dressed in purple who had helped me return to my own time.

Powerful, indeed.

Although the woman before me seemed to have tapped into something very real from my past, she was also talking to other humans about things like "dark energy" and "curses." I didn't want to open myself up to those lower vibrations, so I politely excused myself from that conversation.

I did, however, close my eyes and ask that any energy not in my best and highest good be removed, and I thought of the lady from the elevator. Almost immediately, the lady from Connecticut said the dark energy had cleared and thanked me for helping. And, thanks to her, I got one more piece to the puzzle of my time travel experience and brief visit to a place called the Oasis Bar and Grill.

The final pieces of the puzzle were still years away, so for now I had to focus on my own personal growth. Rather than let the mystery cloud my course, I returned home from the convention with a renewed zeal for becoming a more skillful healer.

After months of steadily expanding my business, the time for me to make my quantum leap was rapidly approaching. I was still in my tiny, shared office when a client told me about new offices that were being built at the Galleria, a shopping and business center so large and exclusive that it's considered an international destination.

The next day, I went to have a look and fell in love with the place before I even went inside. The office was in Galleria Tower 1, an utterly spotless building, sleek yet classic, and made of granite. The entrance was huge, giving anyone who walked through those doors a feeling of grandeur. There was even valet parking, which I knew my clients would love.

I walked in and took the elevator up to the 21st floor, where the new offices were being built. The moment I stepped off the elevator, a thought that I had been craving for years suddenly struck me.

Wow, I'm not in Texas anymore.

It had that Silicon Valley vibe, and a tone of amenities for my clients to enjoy. The kitchens were expansive and modern with espresso machines, organic teas, beer on tap, Kombucha (my favorite), and the list goes on. There were plenty of young, hip people inhabiting the space with great energy. My people were here, and I had just confirmed that I could have a little bit of New York or California in my corner of Texas.

The entire floor was open concept, with only fogged privacy glass between offices. This allowed the energy to flow freely throughout the common areas while still granting me a private area with energetic and physical boundaries, in which I could do my work. It was perfect.

A one-person office was five hundred dollars per month, but I *really* wanted a two-person set up. If I moved forward with that, I would have to pay double for the extra space. I'm the kind of person that sometimes wants to sit at a desk in a chair, and other times prefers the nice and cozy feel of a comfy chair. The extra room would allow me the space for all of that, plus a bookshelf. Depending on where I sat with clients, I could set different energies for different meetings.

Still, a thousand dollars per month seemed pretty steep, and I entered the "one day" mindset.

Maybe next year I can spend that kind of money.

Still, I measured all of the two-person offices, selected my favorite, and left pretending like I was going to move forward, even though I planned on resisting.

Once I made it back down to the parking garage, I thought, *this is ridiculous. If I want to meet my goals, why don't I just step in?* Looking around, I saw that this was an opportunity for me to share a driveway with Chanel, Neiman Marcus, and Saint Laurent. There was so much money being exchanged on this city block every single day, and there was no other place in the city where I could have a small space of my own while still being in that money frequency.

The laws of the universe would only serve me in proportion to how I served them. If I wanted people to invest in me, I had to be willing to invest in myself and my business. Of course, there are wise and unwise ways to spend money in order to make it. It wasn't like I was saying, "Okay, I want to make money so I better go on a shopping spree." I felt this would be spending in a way that opened a channel to receive.

So, I made the commitment! I signed in November for a January move in date, and set the goal:

This month I'm going to make enough money to pay rent for all of next year.

That way, I could just stop thinking about it—put it completely out of my mind. Applying my teachings, I met my goal and beyond.

My resistance to money drifted away like leaves in the wind. As I stood in my value, others recognized it too which meant more clients investing in me at a higher level. As I created more and more success, it was interesting to notice how the people closest to me responded. Some who celebrated my accomplishments were inspired to go to new levels also; others weren't so accepting. My circles began to shift, and following my departure from corporate, I began to notice and understand a very interesting human phenomenon.

We humans have become really good at feeling bad. We are more comfortable in chaos and lack than we are feeling joy for a sustained period of time. We are happy for a moment and then upper limits of doubt and fear arise, and we self-sabotage.

I was on constant lookout for my upper limits and limiting beliefs, and I challenged myself to go beyond where traditional thinking would take me. I wanted the quantum leaps; I didn't want to build a business step by step or dollar by dollar.

It was exactly a year to the day since I had left corporate, and I was right where I wanted to be. Finally, I was doing the kind of work I was meant to do—serving as a channel to heal people and pets and helping my clients monetize their passion. Unlike the one month that Dharma helped me hit $20k, this level was larger and sustainable.

Of course, no journey is ever complete. Now that I had

reached this new and higher vibration, I was met by external resistance from an unexpected place: My family.

I've learned that when people hear you talk about something or see you accomplish something that they don't believe is possible for them, they have a tendency to make it wrong. No judgment from me here; this reaction is human, and I am not immune. It goes back to basic survival and the need to be right.

Some of their resistance was based on envy, other parts from arbitrary limiters they applied to what was the "right" amount of money. At times, their mildly discouraging words were truly said with the best intentions. When my mother said, "Well, if you get to be too big and famous, you're opening yourself up for criticism from everyone," I realized that much of her fear was coming from the maternal instinct to protect me.

Family dynamics and arbitrary upper limits like these can make for some funny stories. Especially when it comes to handbags ...

In my family, it was considered perfectly acceptable to own handbags that cost three, four, or even five hundred dollars. However, when it became known that I treated myself to a handbag that cost several thousand dollars, this was taking it too far. It seemed that, in my family, Coach and Kate Spade bags were acceptable purchases; Louis Vuitton and Chanel were not. It's a great example of something that is neither good nor bad but is judged to be wrong by others because of their own arbitrary rules.

"Do you think you're getting a little greedy?"

"No purse is worth *that* much. That's ridiculous."

"Who do you think you are that you need such an expensive bag?"

"Very few people go out and become millionaires. You

can lose that money as quick as you made it. You better be careful how you're spending it."

. . . and on, and on.

Little did they know, I had actually bought two Louis Vuitton bags—one was a tote with cats and dogs on it. I mean seriously, how could I resist?

Okay. This is opulent. This is my frequency. This is where I want to be.

It was a gift without guilt for myself, earned not only by hard work but making the best decision for me and stepping in fully. I had officially made a quantum leap, and I was happy about my success—and my LV handbags. It really wasn't any of my business if other people in my life were comfortable with my accomplishments or purchases.

Committed to doing the internal work, I knew if I was noticing jealousy and competition around me, there must be an equally low vibe inside me, too. This became crystal clear when I ended up getting kicked out of a networking group in which I was very involved. The founder removed me from the group for being "too successful."

It happened over a two-minute phone call with her, the founder. She immediately asked, "You've been very successful in my group, haven't you?"

"If you're asking if I have clients that are members of the group . . . yes. I've been active in the group for almost two years and have served in many leadership capacities. I've built deep relationships with members, and in the last couple months, I've started getting clients and referrals from the group."

"Well, your membership is terminated effective immediately, and you're no longer welcome at meetings. I've already removed you from all online groups."

I know, you're probably thinking, "Isn't growing your

business the point of networking?" That was exactly my question, which I asked her right away. The response I received was less than helpful.

"This is not a discussion. It's a decision, and it belongs to me and only me."

The truth hit me like a lightning bolt. I realized there was a seed in me that wondered if I was making too much money—probably stemming from my family questioning my lavish handbag purchases and my desire to belong. Every month I was making more than I ever made as a lawyer, and eventually my monthly sales surpassed my husband's executive salary. Old beliefs crept in, and it's no wonder I pulled in a networking group that removed me for my success. Thank you, Universe, message received.

I went to work, clearing my limiting beliefs and energy . . . and my human had to send some forgiveness and gratitude to the leaders of the networking group because I certainly had a few human moments where I made them wrong and judged them for how they interacted with me. There's always a gift in the pain, and I see now how that was the best possible thing that could have happened to me—it required me to go internal to reach a new level of clarity and confidence.

I owe the woman who kicked me out of the group a great deal of gratitude. Interestingly, my disappearance from the group resulted in crowds of people, many of whom I had never even met, coming to my events because they wanted to stay connected with me. I don't think it was the group organizer's intention to expand my business to a whole new level, but that's exactly what happened. The same month I was removed from the group, I broke through a major sales goal and have continued to grow in leaps and bounds every month since. I realized that I couldn't create the level of success I desired while I was stuck in the competition and drama that trickled down from the leaders.

When we ask for quantum leaps, the Universe sometimes shifts certain things to create space for our growth—it might not feel good in the moment, and we might not understand the reason until later, but I promise it's a stepping stone leading to our highest good. Believe it or not, being removed from the group actually brought me closer to the members of the group. I had no idea how many beautiful souls from that group knew me, loved me, and trusted me; I learned I had friends and supporters I wasn't even aware of.

Reaffirmations of my worth were also showing up in the form of returning clients. The results I was helping them realize were of enough value that they wanted to continue working with me. My first client, Anna, soon returned to me with a pet problem—my specialty.

She had grown up in an affluent neighborhood, where appearances are very important. Life was going great, and she was excited to be preparing for the family's big move back to Massachusetts. Her husband departed to start his new job and prepare their new home for a landing, and she was left with their son, Poodle, and bunny. Suddenly and without reason, Anna's dog started humping everyone he could get his paws on, including Anna. With Paulie the Poodle being a rather large dog and my client being a petite woman, calling the situation "dire" might be appropriate.

Whenever she had company, she was mortified. With the importance she placed on her appearance and Paulie's non-discriminating interest in her guests, she knew she had to do something. She had purchased Paulie from a reputable breeder and hired the best possible trainers for him long ago. None of that seemed to be helping now.

After I got the call, I did a remote session with Paulie to sort out what was going on with him and his humping.

I quickly learned that Paulie was a complex dog, and he let out a lot of thoughts before we got to the root of the issue.

"Mom isn't introducing me anymore," he said. "She's been preoccupied as usual, but it's been much worse recently. Before, people would come to the house and she would make such a huge deal out of me. Now all she does is shoo me away."

That was it. Anna was so tied up with packing up the house, so focused on moving, that she wasn't giving her fur baby as much attention as she used to. Paulie had taken matters into his own hands and decided to get the attention he craved no matter what it took.

"So, what do you want her to do?" I asked Paulie.

"When people come to the door, I want her to greet them, introduce me, then throw my ball down the hall. If she does that, I'll go lay in my bed."

Once again, my client was shocked with the simplicity of the solution. It worked like a charm the very next day.

Time and again, my abilities to heal were filling me with a greater understanding of my self-worth. Meanwhile, although Raul and I had been working to make improvements in our house and get rid of whatever negative energy it was carrying, things continued to be a work in progress. I eventually got my friend Beth and her husband to come over for dinner, but whatever disturbing thing she saw on her first visit was still there.

"If you want me to eat here, I'm sitting in this chair." It was the only place at the table that would let her keep her eyes on that problem area of the house. She wasn't alone in her beliefs, either. Whenever I'd dog-sit for my friend's Shih Tzus, they'd get rowdy around 9 PM and bark their heads off for about four hours—always staring straight into the corner that Beth wouldn't dare take her eyes off.

It was like the old energy of the previous owner was still hanging around, frustrating and irritating me. Every now and then it would push Raul's buttons in just the right way to push him into drinking again. It would even perform the classic spirit trick of messing with the electricity. Yes, it flickered the lights and TV.

We knew that this wasn't a simple matter of repainting the walls. The very guts of the house needed to be replaced. And, the Universe reminded us of this every time we attempted a minor repair.

One of these reminders came in the midst of a plumbing issue. What began as a decrease in water pressure in our kitchen resulted in needing to re-plumb the entire house. We hired the best plumbers to fix the issue and even installed a full house water filtration system. Yet, in the days after the work was complete, we came home to a flooded driveway. . . twice. Apparently we had more lessons to learn and energy to resolve.

Water in any household is tied directly to the emotions of its inhabitants, and that relationship goes both ways. Some of the house's energy was affecting our pipes and so were the various issues that Raul and I were having in our lives. It was like an endless feedback loop of negativity.

It was another challenge that I had yet to rise above, but having undergone such a profound change since leaving corporate, I was better equipped than ever to handle the heavy energy in our home. I could help heal pets and people, why not homes, too?

There are, of course, some things that we don't yet know how to heal. No matter how much you build your intuition, no matter how skilled you become in your craft, there will always be that time when nature must take its course. In the middle of this year of growth, before I even made it into my new office, that time had arrived for Kaspi.

CHAPTER 10

Kaspi's Choice

❧

THE WARNING SIGNS started to show in the beginning of August 2017. Kaspi was never much of a barker. Sure, my husband had taught her to "talk" for treats, but otherwise she was not a boisterous dog. I knew something was going on when she took to sitting across the room from me and barking nonstop. When I watched her, I realized that she wasn't barking at me but through me. There was something behind me that only she could see, and I felt that presence, too. My intuition told me that it was either my grandma or one of my old dogs—Maggie or Bailey seemed most likely—but I had no way of knowing for sure.

Symptoms of dementia started to set in. She was mixing up days and nights. Instead of wanting her daily outside playtime at 3 PM, she would rush to the door at 3 AM. Instead of barking for food at 4 PM, she was starting to do it at noon. Sometimes, her eyes would glaze over and I could tell she wasn't even there in her own body. It was as though she was going back and forth between this dimension and the next.

Growing increasingly concerned, I started scanning her for issues. Time and time again, I kept feeling some kind of energetic congestion in her abdomen. Something inside of her was going wrong. I needed more specifics about what exactly the problem was, so I started pushing for us to take her to the vet. Even though Kaspi was doing nothing out of the ordinary other than barking more than usual, Raul trusted my intuition enough to follow my lead.

When we got to the vet, I figured I would save us valuable time by explaining the situation from my perspective in plain English. "Look," I said. "I'm weird. I can see some sort of congested energy . . . something in her abdomen."

The vet did their own kind of scan, feeling around her abdomen and doing blood work. They were unable to feel any irregularities and the blood work came back normal. So, we did the only thing we could do—took her home and went right on loving her.

About a week later, I was working from home when Kaspi doubled down on her strange behavior. I keep my desk pulled back into a corner and facing the openness of the room, which usually meant I could keep an eye on Kaspi. Now, she was putting a tremendous amount of effort into wedging herself between my chair and the corner of the room, intertwining herself with me. It was like she couldn't possibly get close enough.

Every now and then, she would crawl out from what was undoubtedly an uncomfortable position, only to stand in front of my desk and bark at me, non-stop. Neither food nor belly rubs calmed her.

Every time she performed this little bizarre ritual of hers, I was getting increasingly strong intuitive hits. I just kept hearing, "her spleen." It was more evidence to support my earlier scan. Something was wrong, and it had nothing to do with her brain like last time. That part of her was mostly cleared thanks to the work I was putting into healing her and myself.

"I think she's leaving us," I told Raul that night.

"What do you mean? You just had her at the vet. She's fine."

I shook my head. "She feels like a burden. She knows she's distracting us and keeping us up at night. You have to stop drinking completely, and I have to get serious about my business. She's saying goodbye. She's going to leave us so that we can each deal with our own stuff. She doesn't want to see us like this any longer."

Knowing the truth wasn't easy; it didn't make me happy, but somehow it felt okay. It felt as though, no matter what, things were going to work out in the end.

Kaspi slept right next to me that night, her head on my pillow. Before we went to bed Kinley came up and said goodbye in her own way. She gave Kaspi sweet nudges with her nose and doggy kisses before going off to lie at the foot of the bed. Raul slept in the guestroom because he didn't want to disturb Kaspi; she shared my pillow the entire night.

The next morning, I could tell that she barely turned in her sleep. It was the first night in a while that she didn't wake us up at 3 AM for a stroll in the yard or an extra bite of kibble. When I called her, she only slightly turned her head to acknowledge me.

"Raul," I said, waking him. "Get the peanut butter."

"Why?"

"Because if we put peanut butter in front of her and she doesn't eat it then we know she's dying." The test wasn't necessary, but I still wanted to perform it. Inside, my intuition was shouting at me. "Her spleen. So much blood. Something is happening."

When Raul brought the peanut butter into the room, Kaspi turned away from it. She must have been lying right at death's door. This time, once we got her to the vet, we received a diagnosis that was more in tune with my own scans. Overnight, Kaspi's spleen had ruptured. She was now almost thirteen years old, and the vet professed that there was nothing they could do for her. There was no surgery that could save her. A year and a half after her seizure, Kaspi's chance of survival had been reduced to zero. We were told that within the next twenty-four hours, our little girl would be passing on. We could put her through considerable pain by keeping her alive as long as possible, or put her to sleep so she could go peacefully.

We chose the latter option.

They brought us into a different kind of waiting room. It was private, warm, and comfortable. We were no longer waiting for a diagnosis; we were waiting to grieve. But why didn't I feel that way? It was like a part of my intuition was telling me that this wouldn't be the end, but how could that be?

We'd brought Kinley with us because even when we left the house I knew that this was the trip to the vet that Kaspi wouldn't be returning from. They gave Kaspi a strong painkiller, and she snuggled into a blanket. We spent a little while with her before calling the vet back in. Kinley lay beside Kaspi as close as she could get; Raul and I did the same. When the vet returned, the rest happened in what seemed like a blink. Kaspi was given a shot, and seconds later she closed her eyes never to open them again. It was a serene passing.

Little Nurse Kinley wandered over and smelled Kaspi's face. She tugged the blanket away with her mouth to smell Kaspi's stomach and tail. After looking at us for a moment, she became fixated with the area of space just above Kaspi. I thought back to the experience I had with my grandma and realized that Kinley must have just seen the same thing.

She had watched Kaspi leave her physical body.

After that, just like me with my grandma, Kinley knew that Kaspi was no longer in the room—only the carbon-based shell remained. She walked over to the door and stood there facing it without even turning back to look at us. She was ready to go home, and only once we completed the drive home and walked in the door did Kinley start to cry. Seeing her sister's departure had been one thing, coping with the emptiness that she had left behind was another. She lay in Kaspi's bed and wailed for a full week after that day. Her cries sounded almost human. Before Kaspi's death, Kinley looked her age and didn't have even one gray hair on her muzzle. After that single week of crying, her face turned almost completely white; the grief aged her beyond her years.

My unexpected feeling of peace persisted through all of this. Of course, I was sad and missed Kaspi terribly. Yet, I had a strange feeling that all of this was going according to plan.

As things would turn out, another major change was heading my way and this time it would be statewide. Harvey was the name they gave to the category four hurricane that hit us a little over a week later, dumping something like fifty inches of rain right on our doorstep. While much of Houston was underwater, our house remained safe and dry; our neighborhood was an island amidst a nightmare, and I know Kaspi was watching over us. I don't think Kaspi's passing before that storm was a coincidence.

Harvey acted as a major energy cleanse for all of Houston. The struggle against that storm brought neighbors together in a way that the city had never before seen. Rich, poor, young, old, Black, White, Asian, Hispanic. You name it—Harvey didn't discriminate. Families who lived in the same neighborhood but never spoke were united in the common goal of survival. Suddenly, the raised trucks that used to bring noisy, revving engines into affluent neighborhoods were wading into deep waters to rescue wealthy but unprepared homeowners. As horrible as the destruction was, Hurricane Harvey brought a great, positive energetic shift to the city. The hearts and minds of many people expanded.

Kaspi knew that Raul and I would get the most from what I'll call "The Harvey Effect" if she left us to ourselves. She had chosen a time to go that was in our best interest, but that wasn't the only thing she had planned for us.

Kaspi's spirit reached out to me for the first time on August 26, 2017, just after Harvey made landfall in Texas. I was in the middle of a remote animal communication session with one of my canine clients in San Francisco when, all of a sudden, I was overwhelmed with an intuitive hit.

There are eight clair senses: Clairvoyance (seeing), clairaudience (hearing), clairsentience (physical feeling), clairalience (smelling), clairgustance (tasting), claircognizance (knowing), clairempathy (emotion), and clairtangancy (touch). I've got seven of the eight, and I'm grateful they generally don't all come to me at once.

Typically, I receive hits through only two to four at a time. For this one, however, Kaspi came blasting through on all frequencies at once.

It was a sense of clear knowing, feeling, hearing, and seeing—Kaspi popped in and completely took over the session. Apparently, she had become a little more brazen since leaving me. She told me that she had every intention of coming back to us, and it would take her just under a year to do so.

"I want my name to be Sophie, Sophie Lucita," she said, just before setting a date for me to look forward to—August 9, 2018. It seemed she had become rather decisive and a bit sassy since passing because she made it clear that she would refuse to go through the whole "suffering and rescue business" again. She would be coming back to a nice family with lots of space to run and play. I received vivid, detailed images from her to help me find her when the date came around. First, I saw a little boy in a blue and white shirt, petting the head of a dog that looked like a Golden Retriever, only its fur was white instead of the common blonde or reddish tint that most Goldens have.

The images bordered on idyllic. Next, I saw two boys in a grassy yard playing next to a tree; one standing on the ground and the other climbing the tree. One wore a red shirt with red and blue shorts, the other wore a black shirt. The same white dog was there, standing next to a bench. Kaspi (soon to be Sophie) told me that the youngest boy in the colorful outfit would take care of her when she was little.

"The dog in the picture is my mother," she told me. "Her name is Moon."

It was a lot of rich information to sift through for just one moment of contact. Hurricane Harvey forced Raul and me to stay indoors for a whole week. Cooped up in the house, we had nothing to do but search the internet using the clues that Kaspi had sent me. It was the only way we were going to find Kaspi's future mom. Raul was almost more into the quest than I was; he went crazy searching the web for a picture that was similar to the one I had received.

Querying "White Golden Retriever" turned up results regarding a specific breed of Goldens called English Cream Golden Retriever—which happened to look a lot like Kaspi, remember she was a Labrador and Great Pyrenees mix.

Getting warmer . . . While the rain continued to fall outside, Raul and I looked through the websites of every breeder we could find in the area. I always prefer to adopt rather than shop, so part of me was opposed to the whole thing. The other part of me (a much bigger part) wanted Kaspi back.

I decided to make an exception for my little girl if we found the little boy and his dog, Moon.

With enough time and effort, we came across a breeder north of us on the Texas-Oklahoma border. A little bit of clicking around led us to pictures that were an exact match to the ones that Kaspi had sent me. She was really trying to make this as easy as possible for us. To top it all off, the English Cream Retriever in the photos was named Luna (which means moon in Spanish)! We learned that Luna belonged to the youngest boy in the family, the boy in the picture.

I still felt a little strange about getting our next dog from a breeder, and later I asked Kaspi for more signs. She told me not to worry; she would make it *really* clear for us. Raul was getting a bit frustrated with me for wanting still more signs.

It was February 3, 2018—halfway to the date that Kaspi had given me—when I received yet another sign. This time it was in the 3D, right in reality for everyone to see. Raul and I were out running errands at Highland Village, a shopping center in Houston. Raul said he wanted to swing by the Apple Store, and I had the natural, visceral reaction that anyone would have over stepping into that place on a beautiful Saturday afternoon. There would be more people than Apple products crammed inside.

NO! I thought.

GO! I heard. It was Kaspi again.

Sure enough, there was a beautiful English Cream Golden standing just inside the door. Raul and I shared a look of amazement before walking over to him. He immediately started giving us doggie kisses on our faces. His owner was a delightful woman with a welcoming smile. The moment we told her we were interested in the breed, her eyes went wide to match her smile. She immediately said, "If you're thinking about getting an English Cream, you *have* to get it from the farm where I got my boy." You guessed it, it was the same breeder we found on the internet a few months earlier.

She offered up their contact information and told us about the family and their dogs. Little did she know, we knew *all* about this farm. Now, it was actually time to use that contact information and give them a call.

Nerves abound, I waited for someone to pick up on the other end of the line. Electric energy seemed to build all around me with every unanswered ring.

Someone picked up. I was so excited that a torrent of words came out of me, explaining who I was and what I was looking for. Eventually, I boiled my feelings down to a single question. "Will you be breeding Luna any time soon?"

The answer was sadly no. "Luna is our youngest son's pet," the woman said.

My heart sank a little bit at that news. It wouldn't be in time to meet Kaspi's August 9th deadline. Could she have made a mistake?

"But our other dog Aspen will have a litter in the fall," the woman on the other end of the line said with hope in her voice.

Raul jumped at the possibility of getting his little girl back. The minor detail of the mother's name didn't bother him. Kaspi had put in so much effort to get us to this breeder. If they were expecting a litter from Aspen this fall, then that must be the one our little girl would be returning to us through. I was a little on the fence about it. A name like Aspen seemed a far cry from Luna.

Still, we put down a deposit on Aspen's litter. We just couldn't risk missing the opportunity to get our little girl back.

The next time I communicated with Kaspi, she wasn't

exactly pleased. She rolled her eyes (as much as a non-corporeal dog can roll them) and said, "Well, I guess I have some work to do," and she left. I assumed she was going to find a way to come through Aspen's litter instead of Luna's, but I wasn't sure exactly what she meant.

This started a brief gap in my communication with Kaspi. The timing worked out because, as I soon learned, I was about to have some big work to do as well. It would be one of the greatest challenges I'd ever faced in my career as an energy practitioner and healer and also one of the most scary and magical experiences of my life. This time, the first warning of its approach hadn't come to me intuitively, but in the form of a haunting letter from my father.

CHAPTER 11

Blood Loss, Love Found

❧

F LASHBACK A FEW months before that day at the Apple store . . .

It was time for our yearly December family vacation in Pennsylvania, one of my favorite times of the year. This year was special like always but for some reason, Dad and I ended up spending more time together than usual—just the two of us. Social outings, family visits, and lunches out on the town—all of the things that my mom and Raul would typically be around for—were being strangely reduced to father-daughter outings. I saw the changes to the ordinary schedule as happy accidents.

About a month after that holiday season when the universe seemed to be pushing my father and I together, things were great. My business was steadily growing, and I was enjoying the creative outlet of launching programs for it. Near the end of one day—January 4, 2018, to be exact—I was at my new office and looking forward to dinner plans with Raul. I checked my email and saw a new message from my dad. My eyes filled with tears the moment I started reading:

Keveney,

I'm not totally sure where this is coming from. Perhaps it is the distillation in my mind of many of the things we talked about while you were home. That's how my head works – the wheels spin, and sooner or later something spits out. Anyway, here goes.

*Always do what **"YOU"** decide is best. Seek advice. Talk to every expert you can find. Talk to those with no other qualification except they love you and want what's best for you. When you've done all that – do what **"YOU"** decide is best.*

The best person to provide advice on a law-related job resume might not be the best person to advise on an education-related job resume. I've heard that accountants are not the best people to talk to about relationship issues. Etcetera, etcetera, etcetera.

Plenty of things I have done in opposition to advice from others have been dead wrong. You won't be right all the time.

Looking back, I can pretty much see whether what I did was right or wrong. What I can't see is what should I have done differently?

What I do sit and wonder about is – what if I had done something the way I thought I should have instead of the way your mother or someone else talked me into, or out of doing it.

What if my company had done more of the things I wanted

to do - but my business partner talked me out them. What about the things I let him talk me into that I didn't really want to do?

DO NOT DO *something because your mother or I say so. Not because the "world-renowned expert" you paid to consult with says so.*

Don't do it because Raul or Kara or Aunt Vonnie says so. All of these people meet at least one of the criteria I mentioned, and can give great advice in certain, and even many areas.

Their advice is invaluable. Listen to all that they have to say.

But in the end - they aren't **"YOU!"** *The only one who is* **THERE** *and is in possession of all the known facts is* **"YOU."**

I suspect that there must be something along these lines within what you have learned in the last year or so. Anyway, permission granted to use the **"YOU"** *advice in your work.*

Love,
DAD

It wasn't just great advice, it sounded like *farewell* advice.

"My dad is dying. He's dying. My dad is checking out," I said to Raul the moment he called to tell me he was on his way to meet me for dinner. As with most of my intuitive hits or sudden realizations, it took Raul a second to catch up. He asked me what happened, and I started by repeating myself.

When I say "check out," I don't mean give up. Rather, it's the phrase I've come to use to describe the death of our physical body, the moment we leave our carbon-based shell. I could tell that my father's soul was transitioning from here to another plain. Sometimes it's easy to look at this transition casually as the natural process that it is. With pets, I'll often describe this as "time to pick out a new sweater" because that's how animals describe it to me. When I help pets return to their families (yes, like in the movie, *A Dog's Purpose*), the animals show me the "sweater" they want to wear on the next go-around. They give me specifics as to the breed, size, and particular markings for the family to look for in their next pet. When our pets return to us wearing that "new sweater," it can feel as though they never left—just like what my Kaspi was trying to do.

Okay, back to Dad.

I suppose it goes without saying that maintaining this upbeat outlook on the impending loss of my father was not going to happen.

I showed the email to Raul. "Holy shit, that's a lot of words for one man."

He didn't just mean any one man. Coming from my father, who often doesn't even respond to a text message if it doesn't include a question mark on the end of it, this email was like a completely unprompted dissertation.

His status as a minimalist speaker carried through when I called him. He insisted that everything was fine (or at least the same) and went on chatting about business as usual. Still, I wasn't convinced. It must have been something that not even my dad was consciously aware of.

The situation was made even more trying by the fact that I had always felt that I would have to be the one to save him someday. Way back when my parents dropped me off at law school, he suffered a sugar attack and had to go to the hospital. From that moment forward, I carried a heaviness everywhere I went. I lectured him on how to eat better and gifted him my favorite health books. Somehow, I knew that at one point, his life would be in my hands. I can't explain the feeling I had in my gut, but I knew it was real.

A few days after I received the email, I reached out to Dharma. I told her that I thought my dad was checking out, her response was soothing. "Maybe he is, maybe he isn't, but at the end of the day . . . you don't get to make that choice. It's not your job to save anyone."

Sage advice.

Be that as it may, a clock in my mind had started ticking. I initially heard that something would happen in three months, then two. The timeline kept jumping ahead until I finally told Raul, "Something bad is going to happen in the next six weeks."

Exactly five weeks later, on February 8, 2018, I headed to a studio to make another one of my regular, monthly appearances on a radio show. The show ran cameras for video streaming in addition to the audio broadcast, and the host asked me to bring Kinley for this episode. We would be chatting about pet products on the show and thought it'd be fun to have Kinley in the shot. Kinley loves people and going bye-byes (a.k.a. car rides), but that morning she did *not* want to leave the house.

She was communicating with me on a basic level, stubbornly saying, "No, Mom. No! I don't want to be on TV today. I don't want to go."

Kinley had a special role to play in this broadcast so not going was not an option. I had to physically lift her into the car to save us from being late.

I hoped that once we got on our way, Kinley would return to her normal self. Unfortunately, when we arrived, she still had no interest in getting out of the car, let alone meeting new people or being on camera. All she would do was sit and stare, she refused to take her eyes off of me.

While planning the segment, we saw that another show guest had her own line of natural pet products and treats. We thought it would be great for Kinley to try them on the air—this was why I'd brought Kinley. Now, Little Nurse Kinley is a total momma's girl, but she normally takes treats from anyone; she is a Labrador after all.

Well, not today.

In fact, I was the only one from whom she'd accept any food. Let's just say her pouting made for a slightly awkward broadcast of digital radio.

After the show, I went out to lunch with the host. We snagged a table on the patio that overlooked an open field. The whole meal, Kinley seemed preoccupied and stared out into nothingness. It was as if there was something she could see that I couldn't. Whenever an animal acts like this, it freaks me out a little because I know they're seeing something and trying to get our attention.

Kinley wouldn't give away any clues until she suddenly broke her gaze, looked at me, and shouted, "Mom! Check your phone!"

My phone was set to do not disturb for the radio show.

When I looked at the screen, I saw loads of missed calls from my mom, aunt, cousin, and Raul. There were text messages galore:

"Call me call me call me."

"Where are you?"

"Call your mom."

Before I could dial her, I glanced at the last text my mom sent. "Keveney, I don't know where you are. I can't get a hold of you. Please call me. Your dad fell at work and now he's had a heart attack. He has two extremely life-threatening conditions that are working against each other. I'm not sure what's going to happen or if he's going to make it. Call us."

I grabbed Kinley's leash, got up, and said, "I have to go."

"Are you okay?" my friend asked.

"No, I'm not okay! I have to go! My dad is dying!"

I called my mom from the road. Naturally, I was in hysterics. I kept saying over and over again, "I'm not going to make it! I'm not going to make it home in time!" I was terrified that I wasn't going to be able to say goodbye to my dad before he died. My mom did her best to calm me down.

Next, my aunt called to keep it going. Both she and my mom knew that I was speeding along a ten-lane highway, trying to cut the thirty-minute drive home to twenty.

"Keveney. Pull over. You can't drive like this."

"I have to get home! I need a plane ticket!" I hung up with her, pulled out my credit card, and called the airline.

While I was speeding my way home and pleading with a Southwest Airlines representative, my father was being treated at J.C. Blair Memorial Hospital in my hometown. I knew it was a humble place, matching the small town it was situated in. I didn't know if they were fully equipped to deal with what my dad was experiencing.

What the heck happened?

I would soon find out that all of this started with a dizzy spell and a fall at work. Luckily, before he could leave work and drive home, his co-worker stopped him. His skin was ghost-white. They called an ambulance and from then on things became a blur for my dad. At one point, he remembers sitting in the ER with a bucket full of fresh blood sitting next to him. He remembers talking to the nurse about it.

"God, whose blood is that? Get it away from me."

"It's yours," the nurse replied.

My dad had vomited up *that* much blood.

As if that wasn't enough, he had a heart attack minutes after arriving at the hospital.

While I drove and struggled to book a flight, I only had two basic details: heart attack and mysterious internal bleeding.

Not a good combination.

"What's the soonest you can get me from Houston to Pittsburgh?" I asked.

The answer was not good. It would be *three days* before they could get me there.

Insanity.

"Okay how about anything between Texas and Pennsylvania?"

They had a 5 AM flight out of Dallas—a four-hour drive from Houston.

"Okay. Book it."

I lost some time on the rest of the drive home; my memory wasn't quite working like it was supposed to. All I know is that I walked in the door with a ticket to Pittsburgh in my inbox. To this day, I have no idea how much it cost.

Raul was there waiting for me.

"What do we need to do?"

"Pack an overnight bag. We're going to Dallas. I have to be at the airport by 3 AM."

I was in such a rush that I actually packed my carry-on full of dirty clothes. Fashion wasn't exactly the first thing on my mind. Once we were in the car and driving, the plan started coming together. We had Kinley with us, which meant we needed a hotel that would let her spend the night before Raul took her back home the next day.

On the Pennsylvania side of things, my aunt would be

at my parent's house to take care of their dog. My cousin Whitney, just like she did when my grandma was sick, would pick me up from Pittsburgh the moment I landed.

Sadly, my father's condition had not improved at all. On the brighter side, though, things were moving as smoothly as possible at the hospital. The cardiologist happened to be at the hospital when dad was brought in, and he was not occupied with another patient. The newly opened catheterization lab was also unoccupied; had my dad suffered a heart attack just months earlier, he would have had to be transported over 30 miles to the nearest cath lab . . . a journey he would not have survived.

My dad's stents were clogged with blood clots; this was the reason he went into cardiac arrest. We never really received a medical diagnosis for how or why this happened. Thankfully though the doctor was able to remove the clots and clear the stents.

One life-threatening problem solved.

Once my dad was out of the cath lab, he was immediately placed in the care of Dr. Keith, a neighbor of my parents and the father of one of my friends in high school. Dr. Keith is a gastroenterology doctor and the only one that stood a chance at stopping the bleeding in my father's stomach. First, he needed to scope dad's stomach to see what was happening.

My mother said he spoke very frankly with her.

"I would never, ever scope someone who just had a heart attack, but if I don't do this, he'll die of blood loss."

My dad was losing a lot of blood. It had become a question of maybe-death versus definite-death.

When Dr. Keith went in, he saw that my dad's stomach was encased in bleeding polyps. He did as much clamping as he could to slow the bleeding. At one point, my dad grabbed him by the arm and said something that none of us ever would have expected—something so intense that Dr. Keith wouldn't tell us about it until weeks later.

Instead of telling my mother what my dad said, the doctor came back with a prognosis that most people fear. "There's nothing more that we can do here."

They were going to have to life flight him to a different hospital to perform interventional radiology, which would essentially cut and cauterize the main artery that brings blood into the stomach.

Fortunately, my mom wasn't going through all of this alone. She had me on the phone and friends close by. It was such a small town that whenever anyone is in crisis at the hospital, all the doctors and nurses look to the monitors to see if they know the patient. As it turned out, the wife of one of my best friends was a nurse on-duty. She called Adam, her husband, and the two of them took turns sitting with my mom until her friend arrived; Adam and I have been friends for over 26 years, and my mom practically considers him her second child. Mom was in good hands.

Meanwhile, I was rushing to the airport, trying to hold up my end of the healing. I told Raul that I needed to ride in the back with Kinley so that I could focus on my own work and come up with an energetic diagnosis on my end. My father's crown chakra had expanded an incredible amount—not a good sign. Just as the root chakra located at the base of the spine is responsible for grounding us to the Earth, the crown chakra connects us to the Universe and realms beyond ours. As we prepare to transition, the crown chakra expands just like my father's had. It was clear he was elevating higher, out of this realm.

Just like I had with Kaspi, I began moving my hands in a paddle-like motion, sweeping my dad's feet to remove negative energy and keep him grounded here on Earth. I had to do everything I could until I was physically at my father's side, which meant working nonstop for longer than I ever had in my life. I pulled out every tool I had. I called upon angels and departed loved ones using every modality I knew, and I reached out to friends for support.

One of these friends was Dharma, and I picked up a concerning theme from her text messages. She gave me some tips on how best to work on my dad, and she offered to support with work on me and my mom. Instead of working with my father, she focused primarily on energetically supporting me, which I obviously needed and was beyond grateful for. A tiny voice in my head wondered, "Does this mean she thinks my dad is a lost cause?"

At the hospital, they were working to get my dad stable enough to be transferred to a stretcher for a life flight to Mount Nittany Medical Center in State College, just 36 miles away. They would be much better equipped to help keep him alive. The flight team was there and ready to go. Dad was completely disoriented and for some reason he was fighting against them. He was resisting in every way he could, thrashing around, and trying to rip the ventilator that was keeping him alive. Being that my dad is over six feet tall and almost three hundred pounds, the staff was having a hard time controlling him.

My mom called to tell me that I had to do *something*. He was fighting too hard for them to take him where he needed to go. Still traveling to Dallas, I started remotely sweeping the energy around his body—the health rays—attempting to bring down the energy in his field and calm him. My mother stayed in touch with me, telling me that it was working.

I hadn't eaten since the lunch I ditched with the radio show host, and even pulling over for a three-minute food stop, my mom would text and ask, "What did you do? Did you stop? He's getting upset again."

I couldn't do this alone. I needed help from a friend, and I knew exactly who I should call.

Michael is one of my best friends and an amazing artist that does amazing work with sacred geometry. It's no coincidence that I have a lot of his art hanging in my home and office. I want his energy around at all times.

As talented as he is as an artist, he's even more gifted as a channeler and healer. When he channels his guides, his voice often changes and sometimes his body morphs. When he's finished, he has little or no memory of what the guides have spoken through him. His ability to channel is something that I call upon frequently.

I texted him the situation and told him that I kept hearing that my dad was working out a lot of karma. If there was anything that could be done to help him calm down and mark this karma as complete, it would be a great help.

Michael responded and said that his "guys" (how he referred to his guides and angels) swaddled my dad in what was essentially a heavy, warm blanket. This would help him feel safe and reduce his awareness of the gurney, monitors, and helicopter.

With Michael's help, I was able to ensure that my father would sleep through the night and do some internal, personal work on the subconscious level.

Once Raul and I got to the hotel in Dallas, I knew that I needed to catch at least an hour of sleep or I would be too exhausted to help in the coming days. I reached out to all of my guides, seen and unseen, and asked them to cover for me. Instantly, I intuitively saw a violet flower, something that I have come to know as a symbol of my great-grandmother responding to my calls. (I learned later that she grew African violets in her garden and had beautiful window boxes filled with them in each window at her and my great-grandfather's farmhouse.)

After that quick nap, I said goodbye to Raul, got on a plane, and kept working in every way I could. Once again, I had the experience of losing time. Before I knew it, Whitney picked me up from the airport in Pittsburgh and brought me to State College so that I could be at my dad's side.

He had a private room in the ICU. On my way down the hall, I kept thinking, *not going to cry, not going to cry. Be strong.* I focused on the positive, avoiding thoughts of what I didn't want to happen and thinking about positive future imagery.

My dad has always wanted to take a trip to the Pacific Northwest to see the redwoods. I imagined us there in that beautiful, ancient forest. Instead of crying, the first thing I said to him when I walked in was, "Hey! Are you going to get out of here so we can go see the big trees?"

I was thrilled with how they were treating him. He had his own team of people and was hooked up to a million monitors. My dad was the sickest person in the hospital, and they were certainly treating him like it.

He was finally able to breathe on his own, which meant the vent was out of his mouth. He was free to say whatever he wanted. A little concerned about his level of lucidity, the nurses would check in with my mom periodically.

"He sometimes talks and jokes about crazy stuff," they would say.

My mom cut them off. "Trust me, he's fine. He always talks like that."

Dad rarely acted like he knew how serious his condition was. "Well, I guess they'll just have to keep giving me blood," he would say casually. He never mentioned the fact that giving him blood at the rate he was losing it was not a sustainable system.

If we challenged him or seemed overly concerned, he'd

get a little anxious and ask, "What are you guys telling me? Are you saying I'm dying?"

Michael and I talked and realized that the less my dad's human side was involved in the process, the better. Bringing him into the healing process directly would also start up his analytical mind, which tended to trigger questions.

Working with clients is typically a two-person effort. The client repeats a specific phrase, a verbal process that both occupies their mind and helps them remove low vibrations while replacing them with the higher. Meanwhile, I go to work on clearing their energy.

For my dad, I was essentially working on him as I would with any animal—doing both pieces of the process.

Even though this seemed like largely a physical battle, I knew it to be a spiritual one. My father's spirit was trying to decide if it wanted to stay or leave. From my studies, I've learned that stomach issues are, naturally, associated with "things you can't stomach." My dad was a person that always had delusions of grandeur, believing that he should have been rich and famous. In their relationship, my mom took on the job of risk manager and tried to prevent him from pursuing what she regarded as reckless ventures. Maybe this was a good dynamic for one or both of them, maybe not. Either way, life had gone differently for my father than he had expected. Now, his spirit was deciding if he wanted to keep that life—even if he didn't realize it.

From Michael, to me, to all of our seen and unseen teachers and guides, to the support that Dharma was providing my family—the act of holding a space for my dad to stay on this Earth plane was a massive undertaking.

My dad was constantly going in and out of procedures, which would naturally be the time I kicked into my most intense mode of healing. On more than a few of these occasions, my great-grandma popped into my energy, calmed me down, and said, "I got this, kid."

When she did that, she would show me glimpses into the operating room. I would watch from above as she sprinkled violet pedals all over my dad. I'm not sure what I would have done if not for the breaks she gave me.

Like I said, though, we were simply "holding a space" for him. The spiritual war within him was still raging and the doctors still had no idea how to stop the stomach bleed. Despite all of our efforts, we were only treading water.

Exactly like at the first hospital, we were given the same dreaded prognosis again.

"There's nothing more that we can do here."

It was time for another helicopter ride and another hospital.

Unfortunately, the weather was not cooperating. Due to the snow and fog, visibility was too low for the helicopter to fly. Dad would have to be transported to Geisinger Medical Center via a life flight ambulance, essentially this is an ambulance with a special life flight team with a paramedic and nurse—the same care he'd receive in a helicopter.

Geisinger Medical Center was an eighty-mile ambulance ride away. Oddly enough, it had been an option from the beginning. Dr. Keith believed my dad required interventional radiology, and Geisinger was the closest hospital place that did it; you might think we would have gone straight there instead of having a stopover at State College. When my mother asked me to weigh in on the choice, I kept hearing, *No. Absolutely not. Take him to State College.*

I relayed the message, and it wasn't until we arrived at Geisinger that I understood why our intuition had steered us away from this place.

It was a nightmare.

The hospital was too big for its own good. The left hand didn't know what the right was doing. Our hospitalist was working his first week on the job, and he seemed completely unwilling to listen to us or read my dad's records. We kept telling him that he should be *very* concerned that my dad's hemoglobin levels had fallen dangerously low.

The hospitalist checked. "Oh, he's fine. When you're in a hospital you drop pretty low before you have to worry."

Maybe he was right when it came to otherwise healthy patients, but the cardiologist told us it was life-threatening to drop that low for someone who just had a heart attack.

"Well, shit," the hospitalist actually said. "When did he have a heart attack? How many years ago?"

My mom and I looked at each other before simultaneously screaming, "Three days ago!"

At least the nurses were on our side. One actually went as far as telling me that if we had come here directly from J.C. Blair that my dad wouldn't be alive—"The politics, red tape, and wait time would have killed your dad," she said.

Thank you, intuition.

That same nurse, having seen me work, pulled me aside and asked me, "Are you a witch?"

I laughed. "No. I'm a channel for healing."

"Can you talk to dead people? I think I have a ghost in my house. Do you think you could get him to leave?"

I had to let her down easy on that one, although I really appreciated her curiosity.

Not everyone on staff was as open-minded. The hospitalist (my new Bane) was continuing to hurt the situation and my dad. He insisted that my dad stand up and walk to the bathroom, despite the fact that he was dizzy and dangerously low on blood.

Two petite nurses, trying to "follow orders" as it were,

attempted to help my dad out of bed. Of course, the hospitalist watched and didn't help. I'm sure he was fearful of a lawsuit. Sure enough, my dad fell backwards and hit his head on the bed because he was so dizzy and light-headed.

My mom just looked at the hospitalist and said, "I have nothing to say."

That wasn't exactly true because as one of the nurses pulled me out into the hall for a talk, my mom was letting her opinion about him be known to the staff.

Out in the hall, the nurse told me that we needed a new hospitalist and a patient advocate. She went to get us an advocate immediately. Hearing a particularly loud shriek from my mother, the nurse leaned in. "When the new hospitalist gets here, I think you need to be the one to talk to him. Your mother is too emotional right now."

No, really?

"Don't worry," she added. "I told everyone that you're an attorney and a witch, so they're all scared of you."

I didn't bother reminding her that I was neither a witch nor licensed to practice law in Pennsylvania.

They did two more stomach scopes at Geisinger. As with all previous procedures, my great-grandma showed up to give me a hand, and I watched with glee as she spread her violet petals all over my father and the O.R.

When my dad was wheeled out after the second procedure, he was drawing squares in the air with his hands and speaking in what at first seemed like total nonsense.

"Tomato, cucumber, lemons, flowers, fire, onions."

He let us sit in total confusion for a short while before explaining himself.

"I'm going to build a garden and have a fire pit."

That was a much better sign than it appeared to be. These weren't just the musings of a drugged and dying man.

Everything he was saying meant he was winning his spiritual war. Part of him wanted to stay.

We were coming up on a week at Geisinger and my dad still hadn't received the interventional radiology that was supposed to sever the main artery leading to his stomach. Whenever we asked, we were told he wasn't ready for the procedure. My dad went right on with his casual approach to the whole situation. "More blood, I guess. They'll just have to keep giving me more. Hey, I'm hungry by the way."

He had every reason to be hungry; it had been days since he had eaten. Still, my mother just looked at him and said, "You're lying here with a bleed, could die any minute, no one has a plan to fix it, and you're thinking of food? Really?"

With his spiritual war reaching a turning point, I continued to spend days in the room with my dad. During that time, I could easily see the direct effects of the work I was doing. He was hooked up to countless monitors, and anytime his blood pressure, heart rate, or oxygen dropped, I would just go in and start sweeping and working on health rays. Within seconds, everything would balance out.

This confused some of the nurses and reinforced the belief in others that they had a genuine witch stalking the halls. The buzzer would go off and they would come rushing down the hall. By the time they got into the room, everything would return to normal.

My mother spent a lot of time talking about how little control we had over the situation, and there were times I agreed with her. I felt like I had no idea what was going to happen. After the experience with the monitors, though, I was filled with confidence. We did have control over how things were going to shake out.

I was still in regular contact with my helping friends. At one point, I had been working so long and consistently that Dharma insisted that I take a break. "You have to go eat.

Get some potatoes, something that is going to ground you."
She seemed to sense that I was on the verge of a sudden
reversal and total breakdown, and you know what? She was
right.

Once I gave myself a second to breathe and eat, everything seemed to snap.

He's not going to make it.

He's going to leave us.

He's moving on.

In the haze of that incredibly unpleasant experience, an
intuitive hit came to me. It said, "Look for the malachite.
Look for the malachite."

Based on my experience with Kaspi, I knew malachite
to be the emerald green, sparkly stone associated with the
Archangel Raphael, whom I had already been calling upon
a great deal.

Around that time, Michael also received an intuitive hit
that as soon as the new hospitalist came in, everything would
be okay. When he arrived, I immediately saw something that
coincided with Michael's hit. There was a beautiful green
energy around him. He reached out to shake my hand and
introduce himself.

"Hi, I'm Dr. Malachi."

"Really? Did I hear that right? Your name is Dr.
Malachi?"

Well, that's good to know!

Things were shifting.

Dr. Malachi got the interventional radiology team to
take a look, then explained the problem to us. It was a classic
Catch 22.

The cardiologist wanted my dad on blood thinners
because of the heart attack. As long as he was on blood

thinners, though, they couldn't perform any kind of surgery because the blood wouldn't clot.

They were trying everything they could to strike the perfect balance between heart-safe and surgery-safe blood chemistry. It was yet another thing that seemed out of my control until Michael reached out again.

"Here's what we're going to do," he said. "We have to reprogram your dad's blood. It needs to be thin when it approaches his heart and lungs, then thicken up as it approaches his stomach."

Michael's guys went in and removed all the stomach lining cells that had mutated and replaced them with healthy stomach cells that had the proper programs. He was told that this would help remove the polyps. I would need to check three times a day to see if there were any new mutated stomach cells and, if so, remove them and download healthy replacements. Michael's guys had already downloaded a mixture of florals, tree bark, salt, and clear crystal light to facilitate with the healing.

The next day, right before lunch time, the doctors proclaimed that although they weren't sure what happened, everything had shifted and balanced and they were going to take my dad down to radiology to give the procedure a shot.

The moment they took him and put him under with anesthesia, I collapsed on the hospital floor—in the middle of a busy walkway. I was wailing, waving my hands as fast as possible.

My mother kept calling my name and telling me that I had to get up and out of the middle of the hallway. I must have looked like a broken robot, hands jerking, convulsing on the floor. I was repeatedly shouting, "He has to be okay!" It was a total meltdown . . .

Until my great-grandma came to the rescue.

I felt her grab my hand and shout to get my attention. "Hey! I got this, kid!"

In that moment, everything around me—the hall, the people in it, the operating room, and my dad—everything bloomed into an African violet. I instantly relaxed out of my broken-robot behavior.

"Okay," I said. "Everything is going to be fine. He's going to come home. No problem."

My mom, who was just dead-set on convincing me that everything was going to be fine, now felt compelled to get me grounded in reality. "Well, if he's okay he's still not going home." She explained that he would have to go back into the ICU first. Then, since he had been on bed rest for so long, he'd likely require inpatient physical rehab. My mother was certainly not a nurse, and their house was far from handicapped proof.

The procedure went off without a hitch. They successfully cut off the major artery that was feeding blood into the various bleeding polyps in my dad's stomach. Within two days, they moved him from the ICU into a regular room and brought in a physical therapist to assess where my dad was in his mobility and how long it would be until he could go home. Because he was a big guy and had been on bed rest over a week, the doctors suspected he'd need 7 to 10 days in an inpatient rehab facility before he'd be ready to go home.

The first test was answering the simple question: Could he walk?

With hardly any effort, my dad got off of the bed, walked across the room, turned, and said, "When can I try stairs? I want to see if I can go home!"

He passed that test too, and suddenly we had gone from "seven to ten days of inpatient PT," to "going home tomorrow."

I think that says a lot about what was going on inside of him throughout the entire struggle. Now that the spiritual war was over, my dad's recovery would be much faster than anyone had expected. The next time I did a scan on him, I found that his crown chakra was significantly smaller and the energy around his feet had shifted, thus grounding him right where I liked him. He had decided he wanted to stay on the earth plane, and he was going to make the most of it.

The next time I talked to Dharma, she teared up. "I'm in awe. I didn't want to tell you this, but when I scanned his crown chakra, I really didn't think he'd stick around. You kept your dad alive."

As I helped my dad get into the car to go home, I asked, "What do you want to eat?" Even though I knew what the answer would be, chicken salad from a restaurant in our hometown called Boxers.

After the drive back from Geisinger, we called in for the food and my mom went in to pick it up while I parked the car. When she came back, she told us about an encounter she had that officially brought the story to a close.

My dad's spiritual war was bookended by none other than Dr. Keith. He was in the restaurant, having dinner at the bar when my mom walked inside. My mom said his eyes opened wide as soon as he saw her. He asked her about my dad and the rest of the family. Then, he told her what my dad had said to him almost two weeks ago as he was being wheeled in to have his stomach scoped.

"He grabbed my hand and pleaded, 'Keith, don't let me die.'"

That settled it for me. Even though a part of my dad wanted to leave his life behind and move on to a higher plain, there was another part that wanted to stay. All wars have two sides, and a part of the winning side had been inside my father from the beginning.

Through all of the procedures, the three hospitals, the drugs . . . he decided he wanted to stay in this life despite not being famous or accumulating massive wealth. He figured out what he would do once his feet were back on solid ground. I'm happy to report that my dad followed through on his promise to himself, and he's now an avid gardener with several vegetable and flower gardens and a fire pit in the middle.

With one major crisis concluded, there was just one thing left for me to do.

I had to get my dog back.

CHAPTER 12
Kaspi's New Sweater

❦

S OMETHING WAS STILL a little awry with the process of Kaspi's return. I didn't hear from her at all throughout the ordeal with my father, and my last communication with her was a little discouraging. It seemed that our choice to put down a deposit on Aspen's litter might have been misguided. If the breeder said they wouldn't be breeding Luna, we at least needed to try getting a pup of the same farm. Right?

As things turned out, Kaspi had the whole situation under control. The breeder soon called to inform us that, for whatever reason, they would be breeding Luna instead of Aspen. Ironically, they were concerned with the prospect of disappointing us when they asked, "Would you be okay receiving a pup from Luna's litter instead of Aspen's?"

Would we be *okay?*

"Um, hell yes!"

Luna and a dog named Max bred on June 12th and the puppies were given a due date of August 14th. I was amazed to hear it—Kaspi would be reborn almost one year to the day after her death, just like she predicted! Fortunately, I had my business and clients to keep me busy during the wait, or I would have gone crazy with the anticipation.

It was now August, and I was at home visiting my parents in Pennsylvania. On the evening of August 8th, I went to sleep in my childhood bed. A few hours later, at 1:30 AM on August 9th to be exact, Kaspi popped in and woke me up. I saw with my mind's eye a tiny, white furball on a blanket. Her eyes were still closed and her fur had the wet, velvety look that newborn pups have. Off to the side, I saw Kaspi in her old form. She was bouncing around, doing a crazy dance, shouting, "I'm back! I'm back! Momma, I'm back! I told you I'd be back!"

We were still five days off from the due date, and my first (very sleepy) reaction was to say, "I know you're coming back. Please let me sleep." I was soon hit with a total knowing . . . it was August 9th! Kaspi, soon to be named Sophie, was *here*. The litter must have been born in the wee hours of the morning. I called Raul, who was back in Texas, in the middle of the night to tell him the big news.

I didn't even have to call the farm to check. The following morning, I woke up to an email from them that said the pups were born just after midnight. It was the end of one wait and the beginning of another. We were looking at another two months before "puppy pick day" rolled around, and the farm opened their doors for new owners to come and pick which pup they would add to their family—and we had first pick of the litter.

Unlike the last wait, Raul and I now had something we could do other than twiddle our thumbs. It was a litter of eleven pups—five boys and six girls. We needed to figure out which one of them was our little reincarnated Kaspi. She told me that she would be the second pup born. When we called the breeders, they said they only knew which pups were first and the last.

Two down, nine to go . . .

It was already clear that she would be returning to us as a female, so that helped narrow down our choices even further. Right around the time we were circling in on our three best-guesses, the breeders called with some worrisome news.

The owners of Sophie's dad, Max, decided they wanted to exercise their right of first pick of the litter. It was a perfectly legitimate claim but not one we anticipated. Now, things felt a little more complicated. What if Raul and I went through all of the trouble of finding which one was Sophie, only to have her selected by another family?

"What the hell?" was Raul's reaction. "We put our money down first. We have first pick."

I took the news a little more gracefully than he did.

"It is what it is."

Later that week, Kaspi came to me and put me at ease. She told me not to worry; the other family wouldn't pick any of the three puppies we were looking at, and they *definitely* wouldn't pick her.

Adorable pictures and videos continued to flow out of the farm and into my inbox. Raul and I scoured each one, trying to figure out which one was our little girl. At one point Kaspi popped in and showed herself in a bright white collar—I assumed she was trying to tell us to buy her a new white one because all the collars she had previously were purple and pink.

The next day, we got pictures of the puppies, and the breeder had "named" them by putting a different colored collar on each one so families could begin to recognize and identify them. Sure enough, one of the girls was wearing a white collar. "That's her, that's Kaspi," I said.

There was only one problem. Raul immediately wanted

the green one, whereas I was in love with the purple one. Neither of us picked the white collared pup as our favorite initially, and my husband was quick to launch his argument.

"This is supposed to be my dog! I want the green one."

That was true, but I told him the choice wasn't that simple. This wasn't just about which dog's energy we latched onto more, we were trying to figure out which one was going to become our Sophie. That night, I turned to Kaspi for guidance. She only said, "Remember, I don't like walking in wet grass."

The next morning, we called the breeder. She said that the only one that was sometimes finicky about the rain was Miss White, the name she used to refer to the pup with the white collar.

After a few more questions, the case for Miss White only grew. I asked about certain mannerisms that Kaspi exhibited in her former life.

"Which one is the clumsiest?" I asked.

Once again, it was the pup with the white collar who could often be seen stepping in her food. Miss White also had a tendency to trip over her own feet more than the other pups and was as aloof as she was present. All of these were very distinct Kaspi behaviors.

Raul and I were so torn that we ended up having a channeling session with Michael. We went into it having told him absolutely nothing, and he broke down our predicament in perfect detail. He explained that if I was single and living alone, the chubbiest and neediest dog would be perfect for me; she had the most lessons to teach me, and his description happened to correspond perfectly with Miss Purple. The same was true for the green dog and Raul; Miss Green was more of a loner and had a great deal to offer my husband.

"If you get either one of these dogs, it won't be good for your marriage. But there's a third . . ." He went on to describe that he was seeing a lot of white objects. "Is there one with a white collar?" He asked.

Raul and I just looked at each other, and Michael explained that the dog with the white collar had lessons for us both.

She must be our Kaspi. After all, Kaspi had intentionally checked out to give Raul and I space to handle our own stuff. In the time since her departure, Raul had completely quit drinking, saying, "I'm gonna stay sober so I can get my little girl back." (I'm proud to share that at the publishing of this book, Raul has been sober for 20 months.)

Kaspi must have wanted to continue down her path of helping Raul and I grow and change, only this time under the name of Sophie.

The final message from Kaspi came as a vision of her old self lying with one of the puppies right next to her face. I couldn't see the collar, so at first this wasn't exactly helpful. Later, the breeders uploaded an image that was an *exact* match in composition, only Kaspi's old form had been replaced by Luna. Still, I couldn't see a collar, so I called to ask which dog was pictured.

Guess who it was . . .

Of course, the choice wasn't just mine and Raul's to make. Kinley had strong opinions of her own. First, she looked at images of Raul's preference, the green dog, and immediately said, "Uh uh, no way. She's too high strung and we already have one of those in the house, a.k.a. Daddy."

I think her issue with the pup went beyond personality. She didn't necessarily want another dog in the house at all. After we lost Kaspi, Kinley was so sad that we did everything we could to cheer her up. Any second we weren't at work was spent with her at our side. When we went out to eat, it was only to restaurants where we could take her with us to the patio. She had been living high on the hog for the past year, and was maybe just a little spoiled.

Eventually, she gave in. "Fine, we can get a puppy, but Daddy takes care of it."

Then, she saw the purple collar. "Purple, purple, purple!" It might seem like she was just siding with me on the whole debate, but the truth was that she's obsessed with the color purple. Toys, blankets, anything purple that she could get her paws on was immediately hers. If I happen to leave out one of my purple slippers or scarves, she takes it and returns to her bed (and supposedly dogs can't see purple . . . I'm not convinced.) So, there was a little bias there I knew we would have to work around come Puppy Pick Day, which was right around the corner.

When the day finally came, Kinley, Raul, and I piled into the car for the five-hour drive up to the hotel that was nearest to the farm. Our scheduled selection time was 9 AM, and we would only have a half hour to make our final decision. My hope was for Kinley to come to the farm with us so that she could make the choice herself, but the breeder understandably had a "no dogs" policy to keep the puppies safe.

When we got to the farm, as expected, the purple-collared pup ran straight to me and the green one immediately went for Raul. I was told that if we decided to take the purple one home, I needed to be prepared for an incredibly needy pet. They might have thought this was a warning, but for me it was another reason to go purple. I *love* velcrodogs. While Raul and I played with our respective favorite, the puppy with the white collar simply sat back and watched us both.

Although Kinley couldn't be there, she still needed to have a say in the decision. While she was waiting patiently in the hotel room, I channeled her into the discussion.

"Purple! Purple! Purple!" She shouted.

After that knee-jerk reaction was over with, she got to looking at all three. The puppy with the white collar had approached us now, and was spending equal time with Raul and me. She seemed like the perfect balance between calm and hyper.

"Gee, Mom," Kinley said, a hint of sarcasm in her voice. "Isn't that what you're trying to do? Strike a balance? Create harmony?"

She was right. Raul and I were two different extremes in many ways. I had grown up in a house where leaving a single dirty dish on the counter might just be the end of the world as we know it; Raul was raised in a house where there was barely a clear path large enough to walk from one room to the next. We needed a happy medium to bridge the gap between our experiences and energies.

Even though Kinley was back in the hotel room, she could tell which way the wind was blowing. "Fine," she said. "If we do this, I want my room painted purple."

I presented her terms to Raul, to which he responded. "I'm not sleeping in a purple bedroom."

I asked Kinley if we could work something out at a later time, and she agreed.

Raul and I gave one final look at Miss White. We could already see just a little bit of Kaspi in her, and we decided then and there that we would be taking her home and naming her Sophie, just like Kaspi wanted.

We finally had our little girl back and now it was time to work towards being a complete family once again. The process was going to be a little more challenging than simply bringing home a new puppy. When you introduce a new energy into a home, there's always a chance it will clash with another before falling into harmony. Like Michael said, Sophie had the most lessons to teach us both.

Learning isn't the easiest thing for a human to do.

CHAPTER 13
Sophie's Lessons, Grandma's Visits

ITHIN THE FIRST few weeks of her coming home, we knew we had made the right choice. The similarities between Sophie's behavior and Kaspi's old habits were abundant. Both would come running at the sound of kale being ripped up for dinner because it meant they could spend the next few minutes on their bed, delicately nibbling away at the stem like rabbits rather than hungry dogs. Both of them even sat in the same spot of the same bed, right leg crossed over left, looking very regal and proper.

The family was complete again, although it would take some work before we started to function together as a single unit. Raul had a bit of a power struggle going on with our new puppy. I warned him multiple times that he was being too controlling, basically a puppy tyrant. He wanted Sophie to obey commands as if she was her thirteen-year-old self.

"Sit."

"Eat."

"Stop running."

He wanted to have complete control over Sophie's level of activity. This was essentially like one person trying to hold down a high-pressure fire hose by themselves—that person gets whipped around quite a bit.

This tyranny bounced back on him, transforming Sophie into hell on wheels. She refused to sleep and would never cuddle with him or let him hold her.

Just a little bit of jealous energy drifted into the house anytime he looked at me relaxing with Kinley on the couch while his pup quickly transformed into a wild child. He asked me why it had to be that way, lamenting over how unfair life was.

"Why is Kinley always so calm? She's a perfect specimen of a dog, and Sophie is constantly eating my face."

"I don't know," I said. "Animals pick up the energy of their owners."

He stared at me for a moment, processing my veiled accusation. "Are you saying I'm crazy and you're perfect?"

I gave a shrug and we swiftly moved on before an argument could spin up.

The integration of Kaspi's new and wild reincarnation continued on at a slow pace. I kept trying to convince Raul to get a coach of his own and perhaps talk to Dharma, but he was in resistance. "You're spending so much money on training," he said. "Why can't you just be my coach?"

"Because I'm your wife," I said.

He did a few one-off sessions, always with a financial excuse for not making a major commitment, until the day that Sophie put him in his place.

He had come home from work and got comfortable by dressing down to only his underwear. All of a sudden, Sophie ran up to him from behind, pounced him, and clamped her jaw firmly around his undies. Being only eleven weeks old, she still wasn't quite big enough for her feet to touch the ground, thus treating me to the excellent show of my husband engaging in a desperate tug of war over his panties as a puppy dangled beneath him.

Every time Sophie broke away she started nipping at him. Raul looked pleadingly at me as I sat back like I was enjoying a night at the theater with Kinley by my side.

"What do you want me to do?" I asked, laughing.

Before he could answer, Sophie made one more flying leap and got Raul's underwear down around his ankles. She started nipping again and Raul defensively turned away to keep the puppy's tiny, sharp teeth away from his manhood. His attacker backed away, still yapping at him.

"Is it safe to turn around?" He asked.

"I wouldn't."

Sophie charged in and went flying once again, this time getting a solid bite on his butt.

Raul let out a yelp. "Help me!"

"Dude, she's your dog."

Sophie, determined to seal off this victory for canines everywhere, wrapped her forelegs around Raul's knee and started humping away. Raul made his getaway into the bedroom, putting some distance between him and the fierce attacker. A few minutes later, once Sophie calmed down a bit, he came out scratching his head.

"Yeah, so . . . what's Dharma's number again?"

We had been told that the puppy with the white collar would be the one with the most lessons for both of us, and Sophie was definitely Raul's teacher during that little encounter. When we brought her into our home, he expected her to instantly become Kaspi, well-trained and docile, with no need to play. Sophie had to tell him, "Yes, there are pieces of Kaspi in me, but I'm still a different dog, I'm Sophie and you need to love us both."

In addition to contacting Dharma, Raul started reading up on how to live with a puppy; clearly, he wasn't taking my word on puppy training 101. He finally realized they needed to play and required a lot of attention. With some work, his relationship with Sophie transformed into a very loving one. Soon, he was playing tug-of-war with her, taking her outside and letting her run in the yard untethered, enjoying games of fetch, and snuggling on the couch.

Let's not forget Kinley. She had her own adapting to do with welcoming a new member of the family into what had been her personal territory for over a year. Raul and I agreed that we would do everything we could to make the transition a happy one for her, and one day we surprised her by painting a purple accent wall in the guest bedroom. She has expressed her gratitude over and over again. She's not very dominant towards Sophie, but there is *one* thing she has somehow made clear to the newest addition to our family: The "purple princess room" is hers.

With that final phase of integration complete, I'm pleased to say that I've entered a new and prosperous phase in my life. I still receive visits from my grandma on a regular basis. Be it from her tell-tale scent of Elizabeth Taylor's White Diamonds perfume suddenly and inexplicably surrounding me, or a random display of yellow flowers or butterflies, the signs are everywhere. Occasionally, she'll guide me into the perfect moment.

Like one morning, after finishing up some errands, when she guided me towards a park just a few miles from my house. I felt a *huge* pull to stop for a moment, take in the beauty of nature, breathe deeply, and appreciate all that I have and am creating. I followed that guidance, an act I refer to as taking inspired action, living in (and for) the moment.

When I got back into my car, I immediately smelled White Diamonds. The moment I turned the engine on, the first song to play out of 10,000+ songs in my library was "True Love" by Bing Crosby & Grace Kelly—a song she would always sing to me when I was a child. The Universe and my grandma were definitely orchestrating my music's shuffle.

My eyes filled with tears when I realized that I had just visited a place called, "Evelyn's Park."

Her name.

I chuckled to myself, enjoying the wonderful sensation of being engulfed in a big spirit hug. She had guided me to *her* park, probably knowing I was working on some big manifestations and that my soul needed a moment of peace and gratitude. My human required a pattern interrupt. Although she didn't speak to me directly, I knew she was giving me permission to by myself and trust that everything would be fine.

Well, Grandma . . . mission accomplished.

Now, I have a space to retreat and return to where I know she'll come through to guide and support me in all of my endeavors.

As if that message wasn't clear and comforting enough, she once paid me another, more celebratory visit. I was driving around to prepare for a VIP day with a client when I suddenly became completely disoriented.

When I came to my senses, I found that I had somehow ended up on the complete other side of Houston. Only ten minutes had passed, and it would have been impossible for me to get there in that amount of time. Without any idea of how I got there, I thought that I must have just traveled through another dimension. Once I got my bearings, I realized I was only a block away from my favorite crystal shop.

I figured I must go in since something much bigger than me had guided (or taken) me to this place. Right when I stepped through the doors, the first thing I saw was a beautiful journal with yellow roses and golden butterflies on the cover. In fact, there was an entire display of products covered in yellow flowers and butterflies.

I knew it was my grandma again, but why? What was she trying to tell me?

It only took a minute for me to figure out the reason. As I mentioned at the beginning of this story, our birthdays are only four days apart. All of this happened right in the middle of those two wonderful dates.

Had she gone through all of that just to wish me happy birthday? No, there was more to it than that. She was telling me that this is going to be a big year for me, personally and professionally.

In my new and confident state, I felt I was finally ready to pursue answers regarding the time travelling I had endured as a child. My logical mind couldn't fathom having a near-death experience and not remembering it, but I was finally open to considering it. The next day, a client came to me wanting to discuss the same topic. In fact, the next four clients to come would all have near-death experiences to share.

Message received, Universe.

As crazy as the message delivered by that woman from Connecticut had seemed, her assessment of my experience was somehow correct.

That night, I had apparently almost died.

Rather than turn to old local history books, I approached Michael, knowing his abilities would yield the greatest answers of all. He had never heard me tell the story. In fact, all he had before entering our session was the question I'd asked, "Can you explain to me what *actually* happened when I experienced going back in time?"

Right away, his guides answered through him, "It wasn't time travel. It was a near-death experience. Your heart stopped and beings from another dimension came to your rescue. Since your body doesn't work like everyone else's, they were able to tweak your programming in another dimension and save your life. There just wasn't any way for your consciousness to understand what happened to you, so your human processed it with a story of time travel."

At first, I felt amused by the way the Universe works . . . I wasn't able to comprehend aliens abducting me and tweaking my programming, but somehow *traveling through time* was an easier pill to swallow?

I had to remind myself that, in this case, it wasn't my job to reason why. The simple truth, on the human end, was that I had disappeared for long enough for a group of students and adults to run around the convention center, searching for me. Michael was the second person to tell me that, during that time, I nearly died.

Who was I to question that?

Today, I'm happy to have shone a little light on one more mystery of my life, although I can't imagine it's an episode of my life that I'll ever fully understand.

We hear these stories all the time and think, "Oh, it only happens to special people," or, "That's crazy, is it really true?" Often we'll just refer to them as miracles or coincidences and move on. I *know* there's more to it than that. These happenings are all around us, and all it takes is being receptive to seeing them. Now that I am present and living my truth, things like this are an everyday occurrence.

As for me, it's been less than four years since Kaspi's 3AM wake-up call. Sometimes it feels like this time has passed quickly and others it feels like I've gone through lifetimes of internal work . . . and maybe I have. Either way, I have realized that the spiritual Truths I have learned to live by operate like a mathematical formula. As sure as I know that a pen will fall when I drop it, or that two plus two equals four, I know that certain action yields certain results and, even more importantly, certain energy yields certain action. Sometimes results come differently than I expect, but the energy always returns, often bigger and better.

I've even learned a lot of lessons from my house. Just like improving my own life, fixing the house took a lot of work, always more than we expected. Any time we wanted to do a simple repair, we quickly learned that a major overhaul was required. Something as simple as replacing a ceiling fan, necessitated that over half the house be completely rewired. What started out as a $500 job would easily end up $20K+ by the time it was complete.

After rewiring the house, replacing the plumbing, demolishing the bathrooms down to the studs and rebuilding, and remodeling three-quarters of the whole house, I'm relieved to say that most of the negative energy has dissolved. The energetics of the rooms that had Kaspi so concerned have improved tremendously.

As for the portions of the house that haven't yet been renovated, I can feel different energy in them at times. If Raul and I get in a fight, ten times out of ten, it will be in the kitchen or living room.

The house seems to mess with Sophie every now and then, and I wonder if she remembers what it was like to live in it as her former self. Sometimes, she'll go wonky and bark at the front door. Whatever it is that she's seeing there, she'll approach it and back off numerous times before leaving it alone. This mostly seems to happen if either Raul or I are out of town. Intuitively, I know that the energy in the house is not trying to do us any harm. Although a certain amount of mystery and mischievousness is still lingering, I'm happy to report that the deep negativity has been cleared.

I know that the remodeling helped, but I'm certain that the work Raul and I put into ourselves played an even bigger role in our home's energetic improvements.

My relationship with money has completely changed. It has no energy, it just *is*. Some months I earn more than others, and this no longer fazes me; I have a new level of confidence and comfort with my sales. In a nutshell, I'm grateful to report that I've more than tripled my corporate income in less than three years. And yes, in case you are wondering, I did meet Raul's request to replace my lawyer salary the first year.

Here's a fun story to illustrate how my relationship with money has changed.

Recently, I booked a high-end vacation to Barbados. My travel agent later informed me that it includes a Rolls Royce transfer from the airport to the resort. I thought, *At one time this might have seemed a little much, but today, I'm super excited for the ride.*

Raul's relationship with money has changed as well. After starting to work with his own coach, his relationship with Sophie quickly turned around. Of course, coaching brings far more benefits than improving pet relationships. These days, he's enjoying the process of fielding numerous interviews for his dream job—positions he couldn't have even dreamed of only a few months ago. The change he's made since the night of Kaspi's seizure is simply astounding; he's reaping the benefits of his transformation.

As for me, I make it a point to marvel at how much has changed since that night, both within me and in my surroundings. My journey isn't over; I'll always be growing and expanding my consciousness. This isn't the kind of story that has an ending. From this life to the next and beyond, there will be plenty of ebbs and flows.

There are certainly areas of my life that are a work in progress, and I don't pretend to have it all figured out. Raul and I have grown tremendously—sometimes together and sometimes apart. I do not know what the future holds for us individually or as a couple, but I'm certain we're both better humans than we were when we met ten years ago.

What I do know for certain is that there are spiritual or universal Truths that are constant and reliable, and I have the power to use these to create my reality. I also know that the second I think I have it all figured out, it's time to go back to the drawing board and get to work on me. Humility is essential; spiritual pride is deadly.

The two most important things that will determine my experiences are within my control: My reactions and my relationship with and trust in Source. You might use the word God, Universe, Ultimate Reality, Jehovah, Brahman, etc—our words may be different, and the energy is the same. For me, the Highest energy is love. We all have a choice, and we can reach for the Higher or not. Personally, I choose gratitude, forgiveness, and love.

I can't help but think that I've come a long way from magic potions made of mud and flowers . . . or have I? Perhaps I'm remembering what my soul knew to be True as a child, before wonder disappeared and I began living in the conditioned box. Perhaps the greatest journey for all of us is really one of remembering.

EPILOGUE
What I Know to be True

Tʜᴇ sᴇᴄᴏɴᴅ ᴡᴏʀᴅ of this book's title is "lies," and we've now learned a great deal about the lies we tell ourselves. The final word, however, is "Truth." That last word is exactly what I would like to talk to you about before we part ways, for now. The spiritual Truths that I have learned over the course of my life have solidified into a reliable mathematical formula of cause and effect. They are not beliefs; they are universal laws as consistent as gravity.

So, what is Truth?

This book has most likely come to you in a time of growth, transition, struggle, or expansion. Wherever you are in life, whatever your current ambition is, it's important for you to believe that there are unseen forces around you, helping you to achieve your dreams. Within those forces, we'll find many Truths.

Nature is harmonious; it is orderly, infinite, and constantly expanding. Nature is Truth, and this is also our natural state. The Truth is this: *If something in our life is not bringing us joy, expanding us to the higher, or creating harmony or order, then it is not real.*

This is the litmus test.

When our energy is clear and we live in accordance to these spiritual laws, we can solve and resolve our troubles and move forward with ease.

This is Truth.

It is the basis for one of the many perfect, mathematical formulas that I use to help countless clients.

I had an incredible amount of resistance to all lawyers back when I practiced law. I made everyone with a "J.D." after their name wrong, and I wanted nothing to do with corporate. Period. I resisted everything about my legal training and law license.

So, how do I feel about being a lawyer now? (Yes, I've always kept my law license active because I have clients that tell me they trusted me more than other coaches or spiritual teachers and hired me because of my background.)

My law degree and experience in corporate has opened doors for me in the least likely of places. I owe my relationships with many of my high-level clients to the time I spent working for people like Bane. In the end, those years spent suffering in corporate had a big upside.

There is always a gift in the pain, but we have to be receptive. In order to reach my current place in life and business, I had to let go of resistance to new ideas and possibilities. Most importantly, I had to release my need to be right and stop making other people wrong.

Before I could receive the return on my time spent in corporate, I also had to forgive myself for making what—at times—felt like an unreasonable and fool-hearted transition. How dare I sink so much money into law school only to turn around and decide I wasn't interested in the career anymore? When we tell ourselves things like this, it only hurts us and squashes our prosperity. Only when I started to embrace forgiveness and gratitude did my career make those quantum leaps. Now, instead of hiding my phase in corporate as a dark time in my past, I flaunt it. Any thirty-second pitch I give, I include that unique fact about myself.

Beginning with this very moment, you can be the victim to your past or the architect of your future. You have the power to choose. We all have a unique essence, a purpose only we can serve. When you tap into that, you become unstoppable.

This is Truth.

I have to manage your expectations, though. Don't think that you can spend two days doing incredible internal work and suddenly get where you're going. We're like a checkbook, and many of us start in the red.

Repaying karmic debt can take a great deal of time. There is no shortcut along this path, as much as you might want there to be one. There is a fast lane, though, a simple phrase that you should embody from this day forward:

Forgiveness and gratitude.

You will be required to drop your need to be right. I know this urge is based on survival and the ego is there to keep us safe. Be that as it may, the ego can also prevent us from ascending to our next level. Embrace the harmony of staying in your lane, find peace in the fact that what other people think of you is not your business. Give thanks for everything that happens to you, even if it seems less than desirable at the time.

Every experience we have, whether we choose it to be good or bad, hard or easy, it molds and shapes us; it teaches us something. Until we have gratitude for those experiences, we will keep getting opportunities to repeat the lessons.

Noticing these lesson loops is something with which I love to help clients. We all have blind spots, patterns that we are not able to see ourselves. Whether it's a type of partner we attract or a similar experience we pull in with different people, these cycles will keep returning to us until we do the work that is required to shift energy around the experience we had and recognize it for what it was: a learning experience. If we don't accept and offer gratitude for the lesson, the Universe will continue to provide opportunities for us to learn it. We will continue to radiate the same frequency and attract the like. When we refuse to forgive and give gratitude, the effect can be very frustrating.

I once had a high-profile client with a world-famous husband. In our first meeting, she told me that she had already been through many healers, teachers, and coaches. No matter what she did, people in her life would treat her poorly. They would hurt her, make her the butt of their jokes, and be their worst around her. I told her what I just told you.

"The common thing here is that you have the opportunity to forgive."

"I don't forgive," she replied. "I get even."

"Then you will continue having opportunities to forgive."

This client has long since moved on from my life. I hope she's taken one of those opportunities by now.

To break your cycles, to end the torrent of lessons, you must take action. Make some changes, let go of old beliefs, forgive, find gratitude. There are things you can do to help your pocketbook, mind, body, and relationships all at once. On one side of the coin, you will be required to sacrifice some things. On the other side, though, it's important to focus your thoughts on what you *do* want. If you focus on what you do want and take right action in this direction, what you want will increase. Energy goes where thoughts flow, what you focus your attention on will grow.

This is Truth.

Many people live by the mantra of "seeing is believing." Meaning, if they haven't seen it, it doesn't exist. Maybe they're thinking in terms of God, ghosts, or aliens. Yet, little do they realize, this mantra also affects their personal, everyday lives. How will you gain money and happiness if you can't see it first? If you don't already have it, how will you receive it? I've found it's very useful to reverse that phrase.

"Believing is seeing."

You have to believe that you can be successful before you can see that success in 3D, before you can see it with your own eyes. You have to first believe it to receive it. And you also have to expect it. We can only receive that which we can expect.

This is Truth.

When we understand and apply the spiritual Truths, life is forever changed and improved. Everything begins to feel as though it has a gentle ease to it, a flow that gives us more latitude to work, more altitude to attain. Getting to a state of flow is a journey, not a destination; it requires discipline and sacrifice and hard work, and it is the most rewarding voyage on which you can embark—and one I believe we all have a responsibility to take. When we align with spiritual law, we open to a new way of being, doing, and having; this is what I teach clients. I provide the formula for them, and I'm able to do so because of the precision and reliability inherent in the Truths and laws that I strive to live by.

We humans have our own subjective truths, and there is no greater proof of this than what we see when we compare laws of the universe to the laws of the land. In this country, we all generally live under the law that it is wrong to take another person's life. We might even say that it's a truth, but it's a subjective truth, not universal. In fact, we've made exceptions to this truth depending on circumstances such as self-defense and state-sponsored killing. Additionally, from one state to another, we can't agree on what punishment is fitting of breaking that law—the difference between a death and a life in prison is a question of geography, one side of a state line or the other.

This is why I prefer to align with spiritual Truths. They are so exact, so mathematical, that we can use them to create our reality. Sure, there are uncontrollable variables. We can't control the humans in our lives, but we can stop ourselves from blaming them for our current status in life. Don't give that power, don't look to the external world for answers.

You are the common denominator in your life. If there is a problem in your life, it started with a seed inside you. It's impossible to create harmony on the outside when there's chaos inside. Your external environment is a perfect carbon copy of your internal energetics.

This is Truth.

If your boss is being neurotic, your dog is misbehaving, your family is growing distant, your health is failing . . . if any or all of it is going wrong, if there is chaos everywhere, don't look to the chaos to find answers. Look inside. Be willing to step into the unknown of the deep, internal work that I and so many others have found to be life-changing.

Remember that we are constantly creating our own fate, destiny, or whatever you prefer to call it. We don't get to pick and choose which of our thoughts manifest. They all radiate and attract.

It's easy to adopt a fatalistic belief system. So often we humans convince ourselves that the external world and the other people that inhabit it are stronger than what lies inside ourselves. Thinking like that—reducing yourself to a mere victim of your surroundings—is a great way to defeat yourself before you start. When we seek power outside ourselves, we become weak; when we seek power from within, we create strength.

New clients often tell me, "I'm doing all the things—the

vision board, the affirmations, the meditation—and it isn't working." They ask me, "Why aren't my manifestations manifesting?"

Does gravity ever stop working? Does the sun ever fail to rise? Of course not. The spiritual Truths are working perfectly for them, and they are manifesting all the time. The problem is that we humans do "the things" in the morning and then go about our day in our human way; we honk at the slow driver that tests our patience, we judge our boss or employee, we gossip with friends, we get angry with our spouse or partner, we compare ourselves to others and wish we had what they have. The vision boards and morning meditations don't stand a chance against all that negativity. Can you imagine dropping fifty pounds while sitting on the couch eating pizza and ice cream? So what if you had a green juice for breakfast? Likewise, we can't expect to do one good deed in the morning and then be in low-vibes the remainder of the day and get what we want.

This is Truth.

Don't get me wrong; I have human moments.

I've been known to judge how Raul loads the dishwasher on more than a few occasions, and I sometimes get envious when I see a young kid fly by in *my* Maserati. Stuff happens, we're human. However, if we live our lives bathed in resentment, jealousy, anger, doubt, or not feeling good enough, we can't expect to reach a higher level.

It's not just vision boards and meditations that create. Our thoughts, words, and actions radiate a call to the Universe—the rich, creative substance that flows all around and through us—and the Universe responds to our call by attracting and bringing back to us a perfect vibrational match. Don't be fooled; thoughts are things.

Scientists tell us that thoughts travel at the same speed of light, which is *way* faster (930,000 times faster to be exact) than the sound of our voice. As we think, we generate a power that travels far and near. This power sets up a radiation, and what's in our mind begins to take form in the external world. Whatever we think in our minds must grow.

This is Truth.

That sarcastic retort or negative comment that's on the tip of your tongue but you refrain from saying it and convince yourself it didn't count because you never said it aloud, it matters. Even if you bite your tongue and keep from saying something that's negative or judgmental, it's too late—the thought and that vibration is already out in the Universe attracting a like frequency back to you. It's creating things, and it's shaping your world. Our thoughts become our habits, our habits become our character, and our character shapes our life experience. Every great teacher and sacred text confirms, "As you think, so you become."

If we don't know how to control this powerful force from within, the effects can be felt in unpleasant ways. Thinking that everyone is out to get us, or that life is hard, or making money is an uphill battle—all of these things will coalesce to make our lives reflect those beliefs.

As humans, we seem to spend a great deal of time focusing on what we *don't* want, and because of that we end up repelling goodness. We fear getting sick or being criticized. I don't have to tell you what things those two thoughts will bring into our lives. Even debt—crushing at times—can be tricky to think about in a positive way. Many people focus on the balance of their credit cards. They've got to get that number to zero, and they fantasize about that zero all day and night. In the end, instead of attaining that zero balance, they end up creating or producing zeroes in every aspect of their lives. Zero love, zero happiness, zero wealth, zero connection to Source.

Don't focus on that practically negative number. Instead,

focus on being the master of your finances. Then, as master, you can choose the number you want to manifest.

It's important for you to realize the interconnected nature of every aspect of your life. Love, money, health, spirituality . . . one affects the others. If you keep ignoring the doctor's warning and smoke your cigarettes, eventually you're going to have medical bills. The money problems that come with those bills will undoubtedly affect your relationships.

It's all connected. We're all connected.

Understandably, many of my clients want the same things all at once. More money, a better relationship with their partner, deeper spiritual connection, lose x-amount of pounds. To that request, I always say: "What is the *one* thing that you're spending the most time thinking about in low vibration? Focus on raising that one, and the rest will follow."

One final trick I'll share with you:

Whatever you're struggling with, if it seems to hold some overwhelming size and power over you, the answer is not to fight harder. Instead, let go. Do exactly what I did the week after Kaspi got sick: surrender. Trust that the Universe supports you in all ways and is the one and only source of all supply, all prosperity.

There is great power in surrendering and trusting that you are not alone; you are constantly co-creating your reality and influencing your fate.

This is Truth.

Rewind to your youthful days, experience the things you did as a five-year-old, the things that brought you joy and filled you with excitement and wonder. Let their energy surround you and lift you higher.

There, you will find the great wisdom you seek.

There, is *your* Truth.

Acknowledgments

I AM DEEPLY THANKFUL to the following people for their friendship, their inspiration, their assistance, and their encouragement in sharing my story with the world: Heather Wells, Michael Golden, Jennifer Johnson, Donna Orbovich, Jennie Fuller, Christina Tervay, Beth Revere, Shari Balouchi, Ginny Phillips, Kimberly Treacy, Tim, and Zarinah.

I am grateful for my amazing clients (human and fur) and dedicated Conscious Conversation HTX community—thank you for allowing me to be your teacher and to speak on spiritual matters, universal truth, high prosperity teachings, peak performance, animal communication, and healing. Many of our discussions and coffee circles helped me to focus my thoughts for this book, and I thank each of you.

To my forever besties who loved me before, during, and after the Lost Years—I know I made it challenging at times, thank you for always being a safe place for me to land: Kara Ellenberger, Sara Sweeney, Adam McBride, Katie Mosholder, Henry Brown, Shannon Fleming, Rosemary Vega, Joanna Clark, Gretchen Barber-Strunk, Dominic Aguero, Alicia Struble, Robin Paterson, Jess Royer Maher, Paula Reeves, Heather Kelly Hanlon, Heather Grove, Christy Steidle, Clay Schott, Chris Deline, Leann Hamman, Joan & John Clipper, John Robert Clipper, Jarmila Polte, Donna Weimer, Kathy Jones, and Sarah Strunk.

I also send much love and gratitude to Raul; Harry Stroup and Fay Glosenger, my parents; Aunt Karen and

Whitney; Aunt Vonnie and the Huneke House; Maggie & Raul Avila; and my entire, extended family. Without your constant love and support, neither this book nor I would exist."

Last but certainly not least, I am forever grateful for my four-legged, furry soul mates and teachers: Kinley, Sophie, Kaspi, Bailey, Mellie, Maggie, Snickerdoodle, and Samantha. Thank you for always dropping me into the present moment, making me laugh, and loving me unconditionally.

About the Author

KEVENEY EVANNE AVILA, J.D., is an expert at helping professionals fuse universal law and peak performance to unlock their full potential in business and life. For a decade, Keveney practiced (man's) law in corporate America. Now, she combines spirituality, ancient healing technologies, and cutting-edge science to create unlimited success for those that seek a higher version of themselves.

Keveney is also well-known for her work with animals and has been featured with O Magazine, FOX, Elephant Journal, and Thrive Global. When her dog suffered five massive seizures in one morning, Keveney instinctively knew that her stress caused her dog's health crisis. Keveney discovered firsthand how pets manifest their owner's energy, and she often works together with people and their pets to clear low-vibration energy and trauma in both the humans and animals.